WHAT I WISH I KNEW
BEFORE BECOMING AN
INSTRUCTIONAL
DESIGNER

BY

DR. LUKE HOBSON

FOREWORD BY DR. KARL KAPP

THANK YOU

To my wife: Karissa Woodward-Hobson

To my parents: Rose and Mark Hobson

To my brother: Joel Dinsmoor

To my mentors: Dr. Liz Bonin, Sarah Cochran, Will Webb, and TC Haldi

To my friends at MIT: James Stanton, Dr. Beatriz Carramolino, Shilpa Idnani, Zach Peters, Franklin Mathieu, Liz Jukovsky, Chris Lanfranco, and Masa Suzuki,

To my incredible and patient editor: Jen Abbott

To all of the members in the Instructional Design Institute Community

To the cool kids: Peter Shea, Dr. Heather Dodds, Dr. Nikki James, and Dr. Pauline Muljana

To my instructional design friends: Holly Owens, Heidi Kirby, Dr. Robin Sargent, Leigh Morris, Dr. Nicole Papiannou Lugara, Sydea Fatima, Sarah Callan, Dr. Julia Huprich, Dr. Penny Ralston-Berg, Dr. Karl Kapp, Seth Odell, Sonia Tiwari, Dr. Dawn DiPeri, and many, many more.

To all those who doubted me

CONTENTS

FOREWORD

My career in the field of instructional design started by accident in the sixth grade. Of course, at that moment, I couldn't have imagined how this field would impact every aspect of my life from my graduate school choices to career decisions to even raising my kids. First, let's go back in time a little bit (actually, a lot).

I had joined an acting class in sixth grade because I thought I wanted to pursue life as a movie star. The class that I had joined was then asked to participate as "actors" in a safety video teaching kids to be safe crossing the street and around traffic. The company that was tasked with creating the video was called Applied Science Associates (ASA). ASA was an instructional design firm (although I didn't know it at the time). ASA did a great deal of work for the Department of Defense as well as some commercial projects.

My big break in sixth grade with ASA was through a project called "The Willy Whistle Safety Initiative" or something like that. Willy was a hand puppet shaped like a whistle who would coach children, like myself, on safety tips related to cars and roadways. I was loosely considered on screen talent. My role was to make sure that I looked both ways before crossing the street as I thanked Mr. Whistle for his sound advice on doing just that.

Fast forward to senior year in college, I had majored in English, almost minored in Psychology (did not want to cut heads off of rats) and had earned a teaching certificate. My goal was to go on to teach as my grandmother, father and mother had all done. But, alas, as I graduated there was a considerable ebb in teaching opportunities and I needed something to do while I looked for a full-time teaching job. I decided to look for an internship somewhere.

As fate would have it, a friend of our family mentioned to my father or mother that some place called Applied Science Associates was hiring interns who could write, teach and knew something about psychology. It seemed like a good fit and since I had worked there before I figured it was a good place to apply to be an intern until I could find a teaching position.

During the ASA interview I mentioned that I had done some work for the company previously. They were a little shocked because I was barely out of college. I then explained my work on the Willy Whistle project. They laughed, told me politely that the Willy Whistle experience was irrelevant, and promptly gave me a test where I had to create a small lesson out of the content they provided. I must have done alright on the test because I got the internship.

After several weeks of working at ASA and enjoying every minute of it, I finally asked my boss "What do you do here?" he replied, "instructional design." I had never heard that term before but I was hooked.

Unfortunately for me, I had no idea what I was doing and I stumbled a great deal. Back then there was no online institute or academies (actually ubiquitous modem-based on-line access wouldn't be available until several years later) so I struggled. In fact, I struggled so much that several folks suggested I go on for a Master's degree which was the only practical way, at that time, to learn the craft.

Fast forward and today there are lots of great resources for learning about instructional design and, in my opinion, you have in your hand or on your laptop one of the best, congratulations.

What Dr. Luke Hobson has done with "What I Wish I Knew Before Becoming an Instructional Designer" is to write the penultimate guide for becoming an instructional designer. It's everything I wish I had been told and everything you need to know, it's a guidebook as well as a story of a personal journey. It's 30 years too late for me (although I've learned a thing or two myself from reading it) but it's just in time for anyone considering joining this wonderful field or even if you are a few years in.

Dr. Hobson has included answers to key questions such as "what does the day in the life of an instructional designer look like?" to "how do I teach myself a new skill?" to "how do I work with a subject matter expert (SME)?" He covers everything you would want to know. He covers authoring tools, learning management systems and working with different internal cultures. If there is a question you have about how to be successful in the field of instructional technology, Dr. Hobson provides an answer in this book.

But he also, expertly, provides prompts for you to reflect on learning—take his advice. Any good instructional designer will tell you, there is no learning without reflection. And there is no learning without practice. The practice and reflection exercises at the end of each chapter are great tools to help you reach your goals. Don't just read this book, use it as a guide and a roadmap. There are so many good ideas and tidbits in this book. The entire focus and thrust of the book are to provide you with practical tips and career guidance in the instructional design field.

The field of instructional design is dynamic and exciting but that also makes it a bit intimidating. A guidebook like this will help you avoid mistakes, focus your efforts and achieve your desired level of success with fewer headaches, wrong turns and mis-steps. Take the time to really understand what Dr. Hobson is explaining and leverage his experience to craft a strong, productive career as an instructional designer.

In my 30 plus years in the field, I have found that the more it changes, the more it stays the same. It's a field of friendly, professional folks who will almost always lend a hand and provide the guidance you need to maximize your career. Dr. Hobson's book "What I Wish I Knew Before Becoming an Instructional Designer," is the guidance you need to be successful and to start your wonderful career in the field whether you are in sixth grade or a graduate student. It's never too late to join the growing ranks and to call yourself an instructional designer.

Karl M. Kapp, Ed.D.
Professor of Instructional Technology, Bloomsburg University
Founder of the Learning and Development Mentor Academy

PREFACE AND MY STORY

W hy write a book? In a world filled with technology, writing a book never appealed to me. I would rather create blogs, podcasts or YouTube videos to share my experiences; however, blog posts get buried over time, podcast players list so many episodes at once, and YouTube will only suggest so many videos from the same channel. Wouldn't it be great to just hand someone a collection of knowledge that they could refer back to whenever they wanted? Well, maybe I should take books more seriously, and that's how I finally got here.

I can confidently tell you that I never envisioned writing this. The troublesome thought crossed my mind several times, wondering, "what if I created this book and no one would read it?" I'd probably sell three copies: one to my Mom, one to my Dad, and one to my wife. Perhaps I would buy my own book out of pity so four in total. You had different plans for this book, though! I can't thank the instructional design community for their words of encouragement with this entire process. From the bottom of my heart, thank you for purchasing this book. Without you, there would be no blog, podcast, YouTube channel, or Institute. I've tried to produce content over the last couple of years based on what you were looking to learn about and your feedback. Your messages on LinkedIn, Facebook, Twitter, and email truly kept me going.

So, what can you expect with this book? The title really does describe everything you are about to read. If you are like me, you have listened to interviews of successful people. The interviewer, like clockwork, will always ask a question such as, "If you could go back in time and give yourself advice, what's one thing you wish you knew about?" I don't know if I would classify myself as a successful person, but I'll admit that I'm a few steps ahead of others. As I chatted with new and aspiring instructional designers, this same question kept making an appearance and it had me pause and give this some real thought. If I could hypothetically download everything I've learned over the years and give it to you, what would it look like? What would I do differently? Would I even change anything or just follow the same adage of "everything happens for a reason?" Honestly, I'm not sure. I have a ridiculous story of how I got to where I am today and nothing and no one could've prepared me for what my life would be like.

Growing up, I listened to a band called, Alexisonfire and they had one song with a lyric that stuck with me, "Times change and people change with them." 16 years later, I still remember the song perfectly. You see times have changed, and I have absolutely changed with them. I'm a Program Manager for MIT and I lead the design and development of our online professional development programs. I teach online graduate courses part-time, and have dabbled in this entrepreneur realm with a blog, podcast, YouTube Channel, and an institute focused on professional development for instructional designers. All of these things are mind boggling to mention as I'm a high school flunk out.

It was my junior year in a small private high school in Manchester, New Hampshire. The school had a strong reputation for preparing their graduates to move on to the college of their dreams. There was a dedicated part during the morning assembly to announce where students had been accepted, to the applause of their classmates. Every time this happened, I sunk lower and lower into my chair, wishing that I could melt into the floor. I hated school. I had no plans on going to college. I often wondered how my peers could enjoy the trivial classes that weren't teaching us anything for the real world. Did no one else seem to notice? Was I really the only one wondering why on earth I was wasting time and money studying about material that would never help me? I had my fair share of arguments with teachers asking about how the content was going to be useful in the future and as you can imagine, these never went well.

My grades started to fall at an alarming rate. Eventually, I stopped caring all together and I was put on academic probation, meaning I had a few more strikes and then, I was out. This forced me to attend summer school, not once, but twice. This didn't improve anything. The root of my problem wasn't that I lacked the ability to do the work; it was that I failed to see the connection to how this education would serve me on my next steps in life. At this point, I completely quit trying. I failed my probation period and essentially had an intervention with teachers and staff. I was hit hard with reality that I wasn't allowed back. After more summer schooling, I had enough credits to move on to my senior year with the public high school down the street.

It was terrifying.

Going from a class of 80 to a class of 500 was the most overwhelmed I've ever felt in my life. The building was huge and I needed a physical map to figure out where to go. Fortunately for me, I didn't feel alone. Some friends I worked with attended the same school and I anxiously followed them around, asking them to guide me through the unknown hallways. But, public school had one other huge, unexpected surprise for me: music classes. I always wanted to be a musician and these courses answered finally showed me some relevance of how what I learned in school could be applied to my future. My ideal college, if I was forced to pick one, would've been Berklee College of Music. My guitar teacher went there and I thought he was living the greatest life with playing gigs all around New England. My motivation sky rocketed and for once, I was excited to learn.

Music saved me. I graduated with straight A's for the first time in my life and enjoyed learning again. Shocker. I've heard a few misconceptions out there that I must be a genius because I'm at MIT. Every time I hear this, I think back to the kid who failed out of high school. For all of you teachers and educators out there who refuse to give up on a student, **thank you**. One day, they might work for MIT.

My college experience was interesting to say the least. Berklee refused to accept me for my pitiful grades and I can't really blame them. This became a trend as every school I applied for essentially said the same thing. While my senior year gave the admission's office some hope that I could do well, it couldn't make up for the three years of abysmal grades. Every school turned me down besides one: Southern New Hampshire University (SNHU). While they didn't offer a music program, I decided to stay in the arts and pursue a degree in graphic design. My hope was that I could design posters and artwork for bands to still feel connected to the music scene.

My problem was that I couldn't get the hang of design. I didn't have an eye at all for art and my drawing talents could be compared to early cave paintings. I flopped my way through two years of classes, and then was determined to change my major. Then, one professor in the graphic design department happened to glance at my work and mentioned how I must be the best in my class. After giving him a totally blank stare, he told me to keep on pursuing design as I had a real talent for it. This was the first time in years that a teacher instilled confidence in me and I ran with it. I lived in the lab every night trying to get better at design. Eventually, I graduated with honors, a feat that my parents still can't believe. My graduation experience, while exciting, also forced me to face an all-time low job market and I made the decision to go back and get my Master's.

This is when things start to get interesting.

While attending grad classes in the evening and working a retail job during the day, I began to question what I wanted to do with my life. I didn't have a purpose, I didn't see meaning in my work, and I was just going through the motions. That was, until a job posting caught my eye as an online academic advisor for SNHU. I had an amazing partnership with my former academic advisor and she had a significant impact on guiding me throughout my degree. I was thinking if I could do the same for students, this could be the purpose I was looking for. What I didn't realize was that this job was going to completely change my life.

When I first started, there were around 30 academic advisors to serve all of the online students. As word of mouth spread about the new online programs and the services academic advisors provided, SNHU's online enrollment numbers skyrocketed. It was impossible to watch TV or YouTube without seeing an ad for SNHU somewhere in there. Every single term, the university grew by the thousands, and my caseload grew with it. Before long, I was working with hundreds of students each term, which led to speaking with thousands of students over the years. I'll always remember the first phone call with a new student and having the opportunity to welcome them into the university. Their excitement was contagious.

While there were several phone calls to talk about joyous occasions with students, this job provided many unique opportunities to understand the struggles of online adult students, something I wasn't aware of before. It became my role to support them through whatever obstacle they faced. Sometimes, this meant discussing time management strategies and studying techniques. Other times, it meant walking them through the LMS navigation, the course content, or necessary software. I became some hybrid form of a coach, navigator, and tutor. Whatever issue they faced, we solved it together. Being an academic advisor made me appreciate and understand the online learning experience.

This passion for the learning experience led me to apply for a doctoral program in educational leadership. I was obsessed with trying to find a better way to serve my students and I knew this program could take me to that next level. At this time, I had friends at SNHU who were instructional designers. I proactively connected with as many of them as I could over coffee chats and lunch outings to ask about their jobs and what is was like to be responsible for designing someone's learning experience. I became hooked on the idea of becoming an ID. I imagined that my background with supporting students and knowing online courses like the back of my hand would help me land this role. However, this job wasn't in the cards yet.

I ended up going through an endless cycle of applying for an instructional design role, making it several rounds in the interview process, being turned down, and then applying for another role. Without fail, I would always make it past the first round of interviews, but then get the denial email after the second or third rounds. After 10 or so failed interviews with the academic team, I received some strong feedback about how I was approaching learning from a supportive/ customer service mindset, and not from a design perspective. I really didn't understand this feedback until years later.

Luckily for me, there was another department at SNHU who was looking for someone with this supportive mindset. My background with graphic design and customer service paved the way for a role that had never existed before called, "Creative Resources Manager." My responsibility was to design and develop the resources for 60,0000 students in the online writing center, peer tutoring center, and the online learning communities.

I was fortunate enough to work under an amazing director who cared about my growth. She was extremely passionate about learning and was pursuing her doctorate in education too. Our one-on-ones became massive nerd sessions talking about learning, covering ground from Vygotsky's Cognitive Development Theory to what skills 21st century learners will need. Without realizing it, every conversation we had made me learn more about the learning process. Conveniently, I was approaching my third year in my doctoral program and I applied everything I learned from my role into preparing for comps, the oral and written exams to demonstrate what you have learned in specific subjects pertaining to the program like research, leadership, sociocultural issues, etc. I studied for these like my life depended on them and utilized an evidence-based learning technique called spaced repetition. I wrote down hypothetical questions that would be on the exams, outlined my answers, and then tried to recreate these answers from memory at different intervals of time. The end result was that I could recall almost 40 pages of information from memory. I knew I was ready and could take on any challenge.

What I hadn't planned on was that in the research exam, the questions pertained to only quantitative or qualitative methods. I studied for months on how to answer a question using mixed methods, an approach of using both quantitative and qualitative methods. With there not being a question on mixed methods, I made the bold and naïve decision to create my own question and answer it with mixed methods as my research method. Needless to say, my reviewers were stunned and berated me with several questions on what I had done. They asked me to answer the original research question on the spot and to defend my reasoning. Luckily, I was able to string together a coherent thought and it was deemed as acceptable.

I passed my comps, so now what?

With completing the most significant milestone in my academic journey, I then found myself looking for a new purpose. With my academic journey wrapping up, I looked to my career for this sense of purpose. I asked for advice from a few colleagues on what I should do next and the same piece of advice kept coming up: move on to another university to continue growing. This didn't make any sense to me. I admired employees who stayed at one organization for their entire careers. To me, this showed a sense of loyalty and faith in the organization. I already had several years of my life invested into one school so why should I leave?

After months of mulling this concept over, I realized what they meant. All I had known was one university. In order to grow, I needed to learn more perspectives and see through the lenses of what other universities believed in to make their online learning experience memorable. It was time to step out of my comfort zone and finally obtain the role I always wanted. It was time to become an instructional designer.

I started to look on LinkedIn for instructional design jobs in the greater Boston area to give me a better chance of finding an opportunity. One role caught my eye as an instructional designer for Northeastern University. The university had an incredible reputation and I figured that if I was to transition to another role in higher education, Northeastern could be a great fit. The job posting sounded not only exciting, but challenging. I knew that if I could land this job, I would grow as a designer.

I submitted my application with my LinkedIn profile and to my surprise, I had a connection who worked there. Remember when I mentioned how I would network with as many instructional designers as I could at SNHU? One of them transitioned to NU and was working as a senior ID in the department I applied for. We had lost touch over the years, but I found her number and asked her if she knew anything about this job. To my utter amazement, the job I was looking into would report directly to her team. I knew that this was my chance and that I had to prepare for this interview like my life depended upon it.

After Googling typical instructional design interview questions and writing down from memory any of the questions from my past interviews, I practiced answering all of them. I created a portfolio, diagrams, and worksheets to bring with me just in case they wanted anything. Whatever they were looking for, I was going to have it on hand and be ready. In an unbelievable stroke of luck, the room I was being interviewed in had a white board. After they asked me the first question, I went right to the whiteboard and started mapping out my answers and showing my lines of thinking. Everything I learned over the last 5 years were drawn on that whiteboard.

A few days later, I got the job.

I quickly gained two mentors at Northeastern. Every meeting I had with them blew my mind as I learned just how little I really knew about instructional design. I was bitter for years at those who turned me down for ID jobs, but seeing exactly what experienced instructional designers were capable of, I realized back then, I wasn't ready. I soaked up everything they told me, from creating outcomes, designing rubrics, building blueprints, interviewing SMEs, mapping activities, facilitating workshops, and more. It was here that I gained some real ID chops in a short period of time. My first assignment was to design an accelerated degree program focused on challenge-based learning between Northeastern and General Electric (GE). As you can imagine, it was incredibly difficult, but I loved every minute of it.

Fast forward to a year later, and I began to notice that something didn't feel right. I couldn't put my finger on it, but

I could tell that major changes in the organization were about to happen. My fear was that I would lose my mentors and be put back into a position where I wasn't growing. In perhaps the boldest move I've ever done in my career, I decided to look for a new role while still being happy in my current job. By chance, I searched for ID jobs on Glassdoor, and an odd posting popped up for MIT. The title was for a "Program Manager" position, but the job description reminded me of a senior ID role. I applied and assumed that I would never hear back.

To my surprise, I received an email asking for a phone interview. This phone call, right from the very beginning, was just different. The ones interviewing me were the other Program Managers and we essentially talked about our favorite strategies for designing courses. The in-person interview delved even deeper to these topics and I was blown away by their attention to tiny details about designing courses. Basically, I could tell they were my kind of nerdy people. I accepted their offer and have been pushing the boundaries of my design skills ever since. MIT has given me the opportunity to be as creative as possible with no idea being too crazy (and trust me, I've had some crazy ideas). My teammates, learners, and colleagues have made me an even better designer and I'm still learning more each day.

So, that's my story of how I became an ID and why I'm so passionate about online learning. From all of these experiences, here are some of my main takeaways:

- Network with the right people and stay in touch with them
- Think about how you can constantly grow in your career and avoid plateauing
- Find mentors who are willing to teach you new skills
- Keep an open mind to learning more each day
- Be aware of your surroundings and step outside of your comfort zone

Lastly, this is super cliché and slightly painful for me to write down, but it has to be said. You can do anything you set your mind to. If this high school dropout can work for MIT and write a book all about making a career in learning, then what on earth is stopping you?

It's not going to be easy. As a matter of fact, it's going to feel impossible some days and you will second guess yourself every step of the way. Imposter syndrome is a real challenge. Doubt is a powerful emotion. Once you get to the top, though, and you get a taste of how awesome and rewarding your work can be, there's no looking back. Your career is what you make of it. Your life is what you make of it.

If you need someone to believe in you, then you found him. I'm right here alongside you telling you that you can do this every step of the way. I know that you are, you can, and you will be great.

So, hypothetically speaking, if I could share with you everything I've learned along my crazy journey, what would I say? Well, you are about to find out. Here's what I wish I knew before I became an instructional designer.

Chapter 1

WHAT DOES AN INSTRUCTIONAL DESIGNER DO?

Imagine sitting in a conference room getting ready to kick off a new project. Every major stakeholder involved joins the meeting like the graphic designer, the video editor, the marketing coordinator, faculty members, and the subject matter expert (SME). Each person goes around the room to introduce themselves. They all provide their titles, which give some notion of how they will presumably contribute to the project. Now, it's your turn to introduce yourself and you say that you're an instructional designer. You wait for the same reassurance from everyone in the room to nod their heads and hope to continue to carry on with the meeting. Instead, you're met with silence and a few people looking baffled by your title. After the dreaded awkwardness, someone finally asks you, "What's an instructional designer do?"

Welcome to being an instructional designer! That last paragraph was based on many, many kick-off calls for designing a new online course and I had to explain why exactly I was on the project. I'm hopeful there is a chance that this deeper explanation of our roles is going to change because of the pandemic. Since the world was thrusted into remote learning and online learning in 2020, a whole new audience was introduced to instructional design and it had a ripple effect on the general population. In my experience though, as an instructional designer, your first responsibility is to be able to eloquently explain what you do for a living. I know that this sounds bizarre, but it's true.

Our field isn't new, though. What if I told you that instructional design has been around since World War II? Yes, our field was created to develop cohesive training programs for the troops. The United States Air Force produced more than 400 training films and 600 filmstrips that were shown around an estimated four million times to United States personnel (Reiser, 2001). You can also thank the Center for Educational Technology at Florida State University and the Army for designing the ADDIE model back in 1975 (Kurt, 2017).

In the 90s, online enrollments in courses truly began to soar and a glimpse of what instructional designers do became a reality (Reiser, 2001). There had to be a position dedicated to building these online courses that students were taking. Fast forward to 2021, and our role has evolved to the point of our titles changing from instructional designers to learning experience designers, e-learning developers, learning architects, curriculum developers, online course designers, online program managers, and more. To add to this confusion, an instructional designer in one sector could be hired as graphic artist while in another sector, an instructional designer could be hired as a project manager for courses. Even though our skills are all based around learning and designing instruction, some professionals side with technology, some side with learning sciences, and some wear every hat imaginable. Understandably, the general population hasn't had direct experience with instructional designers and this has caused confusion around how they can serve an organization.

So, when someone asks about what instructional design is or what an instructional designer does, here is what I say: I understand how people learn online. It's my job to partner with a SME, a professor, or faculty member, and to extract their knowledge in order to create a meaningful learning experience. This leads to designing and developing curricula, resources, and materials that link and align to course outcomes, to competences, and to skills. It's my job to make these priorities transparent and transferrable for students to understand why and how this information is valuable and useful in the real world.

An instructional designer can be classified by four major areas: learning expertise, relationship management, project management, and research. An instructional designer needs to know how learning works in order to create an effective learning environment and experience. Collaboration and communication are top priorities when designing a product. Building and developing relationships with SMEs and managing these partnerships are essential to getting the job done. Every course, training, degree, program, etc. all revolve around project management. If you can't manage a project, deadlines will be missed, confusion will pop up, and you'll face many barriers before the product launch. Finally, research is a critical component to the role. This could mean researching which topics would best serve your audience, what content is the most relatable to the students, or what tools best do the job. Put all of these traits together, and that's when you get my model:

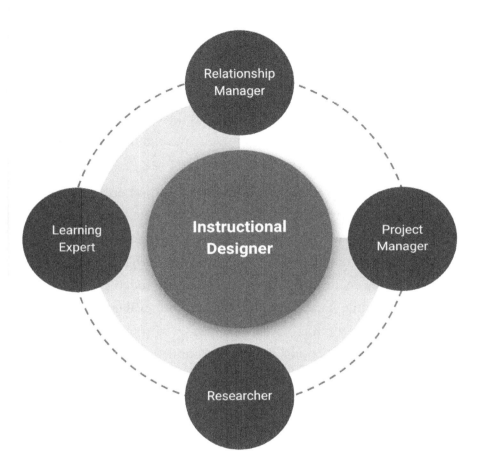

Figure 1.1: Instructional Designer Model

Our roles are insanely challenging, as we are the glue that holds entire projects together. Do not underestimate the significance when describing instructional design! Far too often, I'll hear someone say, "I make online courses." While that's not technically wrong, those words suggest that instructional design is an afterthought and that you aren't a valuable part of the team. That statement is a sure-fire way to have a SME send you a 700 PowerPoint Slide Deck and ask you to magically transform it into an enjoyable and interactive learning experience. You wouldn't say "make courses" on a resume and when you speak about your role, you need to have this same mentality.

To all of the teachers out there reading this book, you are especially guilty of not highlighting the importance of what you do! I understand why because you are selfless givers who cares about the wellbeing of your students. Being a teacher is ludicrously challenging though! There is so much planning, implementing, facilitating, assessing, and evaluating that happens in your role. If you are trying to transition from teaching to instructional design, don't undersell yourself. Just because anyone can make a course; that doesn't mean it's well-designed. Your attitude about your role transfers onto others and they will see you in a different light if you respect your position.

At the end of the day, the instructional designer is the person who cares about why, what, when, and how learning is taking place. Was the training, course, program, workshop or product effective in building and developing the skills for the learners? Did they actually enjoy the process? Could they see the relevancy of the content and how it can be applied from the classroom to the workforce? Was it engaging and interactive? Did it make learners feel like they were involved in the learning process? Could you precisely pin point to problem areas and figure out how to improve them for the next rendition? Did everything I design help the learners achieve the stated goals? These are questions that only instructional designers would ask. It's our job to care about the learning process, the learners, and the organization's success.

References:

Kurt, S. (2017, Aug 29). "ADDIE Model: Instructional Design," in *Educational Technology*. Retrieved from https://educationaltechnology.net/the-addie-model-instructional-design/

Reiser, R. A. (2001). A History of Instructional Design and Technology: Part I: A History of Instructional Media. *Educational Technology Research and Development*, *49*(1), 53–64. Retrieved from http://0-www.jstor.org.library.uark.edu/stable/30220299

Learning Activities

This is your first learning activity of many. Did you think you would be reading a book about instructional design and there wouldn't be some kind of action? It's like I want you to be involved in this learning process or something along those lines. Anyway, expect to dedicate at least 15-30 minutes per practice activity. I do not, and I repeat, I do not want you to simply read through everything without acting. There should always be a goal at the end of each chapter and these learning activities will help you work towards them.

Practice Activity:

- Imagine yourself on a conference call for a new MBA program. You are going to be the main instructional designer for the program. Joining you on the call is the dean, two faculty members, and two subject matter experts. In your own words, describe what an instructional designer can contribute to developing of the MBA Program. Assume that these team members have never heard of the term "instructional design" before.

- In your own words, describe what instructional design means to you.

Reflection Activity:

- Think back to a time when you had to explain your role. How could you word the role differently to make your communication more effective?

Chapter 2

WHAT ARE THE PROS AND CONS OF INSTRUCTIONAL DESIGN?

B ack in 2018, my wife and I moved out of our condo in Goffstown, New Hampshire in search for a house. As first-time home owners, we had many questions and a list of items we were looking for: a backyard for our dog, close enough to a train station, 3 bedrooms, etc. After searching for what felt like an eternity, we came across a lovely little ranch that both of us fell in love with. To make sure it was right for us, we made a pros and cons list about everything: the house, the neighborhood, the city, and the commute to work. With any major decision that impacts your life, it's common to perform a pros and cons list to see if the pros outweigh the cons. I was talking to an academic advisor who was thinking about making the same career change that I did. She asked me about the pros and cons of instructional design, and when I made this transition, I didn't know enough to make this list. Since I was so biased about wanting to become an instructional designer, I only saw the pros and threw the cons to the wayside. Now that I'm a bit wiser, I want to revisit this pros and cons list about instructional design and share with you the real inside scoop.

What's interesting about this pros and cons list is that, depending upon your organization, your working preferences, your coworkers, your motivation, etc. some of these pros could be viewed as cons and vice versa. I came up with one topic that I could argue about being in the pros or cons so I just made a category at the end called, "in between."

Pros

1. Your Creative Opportunities are Endless

Do you enjoy being creative? Do you enjoy critical thinking and problem solving? Would you describe yourself as innovative? If you said yes to any of these questions, you'll love being an instructional designer. Constantly thinking outside the box is a normal part of the job. You'll have the opportunity to design the learning experience for students. This includes creating course outcomes, learning objectives, assessments, and content. You'll create the problems that students will be practicing and trying to solve. It's your responsibility to also map out the course with what students will be experiencing as far as for the sequences of learning.

Imagine designing a lesson plan for each week. What, exactly, will students be going through? For instance, let's say you are designing a section of a week. You want students to experience a reading, a video, a practice question, a discussion board activity, and then a reflection assignment. You can visualize how this looks and make sure the content properly aligns to the learning objectives. You can see an example below:

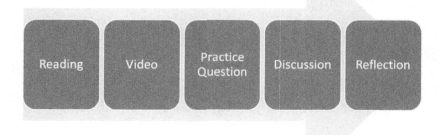

Figure 2.1: Example of Lesson Plan Template

I remember practicing this with a music course I taught years ago and thought that this was an engaging exercise.

Now imagine having this be a part of your full-time job. I thoroughly enjoy designing complex problems with scenario-based learning and project-based learning to have assignments come alive, feel relevant, and equip students with real-world skills. When the world shut down in 2020, I was designing a course on critical thinking skills. I wanted students to have to solve a problem where there was no clear right or wrong answer. I created a scenario-based problem where the students imagined themselves in the shoes of a manager who had a say in the decision of when it was safe to bring employees back to the office. I created an elaborate back story and then asked them how they would ultimately come to their decision. Many of the students struggled with this because at the time, there wasn't a unified answer and peoples' emotions clouded their judgement. I conducted interviews with these students to ask them about the relevancy of the scenario-based assignments and the overwhelming feedback was that they never took a course that had such relevant problems before.

My goal was to create a meaningful course on critical thinking skills, but how exactly I was going to design it was all through creativity. I could say that I wanted to include discussions, but what are students talking about? I could say that students should participate in a practice question, but what should that look like? Should I use a case study about a past pandemic and how this impacted organizations or should it be about futuristic thinking of making new guidelines for the next global disaster? There is a significant amount of creativity that goes into each and every part of designing a course.

2. SMEs are Valuable Allies

Working on a team can be challenging. You aren't always going to be working with someone who shares the same perspectives, views, and beliefs that you do. When a disagreement happens, it takes time to sort through and a level of mutual understanding has to be had to move forwards. Working with SMEs isn't any different, however, it's easy to hear about negative experiences with them. Any seasoned instructional designer can share a story or two about a stubborn SME who completely ruined a project. In my experience though, 99% of my experiences with SMEs have been incredibly positive. When forming relationships with SMEs, it's important to have a stance of genuine curiosity with the course's content. If you view designing a course as a boring task because you aren't a fan of the subject matter, this will absolutely be transparent to the SME. The SME is on the project because of their passion for this subject matter and more often than not, they are thrilled to talk about their experiences.

This passion isn't limited to higher education. You don't need to be a faculty member to want to teach someone else about a topic. I've worked with retired engineers from some of the most prominent organizations in the United

States and these SMEs were just as excited about sharing their knowledge. I may not have fully understood all of these topics as I'm not a mechanical engineer, but I could absolutely appreciate someone's enthusiasm over wanting to pass along what they've learned.

Their excitement on these topics can blend into your own professional growth. You have access to someone teaching you their life lessons on a particular subject that may help you. I've designed several courses on leadership and I've taken away many practical tips from these SMEs and applied them to my life. This isn't always the case with every subject matter, but it can surprise you. I've had colleagues design courses on accounting and found themselves shocked with how much they learned when it was time to do their taxes. It all depends upon how you view working with SMEs and your openness to learning. These folks can essentially become your instructor for the content.

This is a long way of leading me to my point about how SMEs can become your allies. Like it or not, we live in a political world. Your network can directly influence others and change their perception of how they view you. Let's say your SME has a great experience with designing a course with you. The course is well received by students, it's generating revenue, and creating a buzz around the organization. That SME is then going to tell all of their colleagues and peers about the course, the design process, and YOU. Your network will grow with these influences and when you need them to ask a favor, they'll be there for you. I've had SMEs offer me other job opportunities, free advice about a difficult problem, and be willing to connect me with another important figure within the organization. These SMEs can become your champions. This is a pro I never considered until I started to form great relationships with SMEs and saw firsthand, how this can change your career growth.

3. You are Always Learning

If you consider yourself a life-long learner, welcome to your career. You are always learning as an instructional designer. You are obviously learning new skills when it comes to being a professional such as:

- Project management
- Networking
- Multimedia skills
- Research
- Leadership
- Training
- Budgeting

The fun part about this job though is that you will learn new skills in different subject matters and then it's your job to design the curriculum to instruct others. It's actually quite an amazing experience to see your own learning process as you are designing a course. I've designed courses that I had literally no experience in at the time, and then once the course is done, I'm able to carry on a conversation about tiny details. For instance, I've developed courses on supply chain, manufacturing, big data, and more. I had to immerse myself in these topics to understand them a bit better every day. If you find yourself watching the History Channel or an educational YouTube Channel or reading up on bitcoin for fun, instructional design is right for you.

These are the most significant pros that come to mind. Are there more? Absolutely. These are the major points though that I want you to consider. Some of the other pros are remote opportunities, decent pay, and a clear path towards growth in your career. So, now I want to mention the cons, and please, don't be dissuaded from looking into becoming an instructional designer if you are thinking about this career change. The cons are here to provide you with a real-world perspective on what you are going to face.

Cons

1. Your Schedule and Stability

Whenever someone asks me a question about what the day in the life as an instructional designer looks like, I never know how to answer. No two days are ever the same. My work/life balance is dictated by the progress of my courses' development and where I'm at for deadlines. If I'm working on the early stages of the course design process with creating the project scope, the course's description, figuring out who the SME is going to be, etc. this means that I'm not in crunch time yet. This is usually a slower process to make sure everything is in order before the next steps. If I were to describe the week or days before the course launch date, my schedule is completely full. I don't have time to do anything, but focus on making sure the course is perfect before students enter it. With creating several courses at a time, this means that my schedule is all over the place.

One common myth I keep hearing is that the summer is a "down time" for instructional designers. IDs are educators, but this doesn't come with having slower months in the summer. If anything, it's actually the opposite. I'm usually preparing for course launches in the fall. What is true, though, is that the summer is more available when working with SMEs who are faculty members. Since they have more of a relaxed scheduled during these months, it means that instructional designers take advantage of this and work harder.

I've heard from some people about how their roles create a great work/life balance by being able to close down the laptop at 5 PM and then not have to think about work until 9 AM the next day. In my experience, this completely depends upon the organization and the significance of the project. I've had times where I never thought about work on the weekends. I've also had the opposite experience where I worked so much that I had to force myself to delete my Outlook app on my phone and turn off all Slack notifications because there was always something to do. It's not an expectation to be on call during your off hours, but it does happen with urgent requests. There is a certain sense of unpredictability that comes with being an ID.

2. Constantly Adapting to Change

I've already mentioned that trying to describe a typical day in the life of an ID is challenging. The main factor for this is change. As an instructional designer, you wear many, many hats. One day you feel like a researcher. The next, you are trying to create a peace treaty between an upset SME and your supervisor. The next, you are in the studio working with the multimedia team for video shoots. The next, you are conducting QA checks on the course builds in the LMS. While this is exciting in a sense, I've found it difficult to try and carve out time for my other priorities. Since I'm the most creative in the mornings, I like to draft exercises and problems before anyone else logs on for the day. You need to learn to adapt to your schedule.

Speaking of adapting, when creating courses, instructional designers are one cog in the machine. There are other stakeholders involved with SMEs, faculty, the multimedia team, customer support, marketing, accounting, engineering, third party vendors, academic advisors, TAs, learning facilitators, etc. Whenever a change happens within a course, you'll have to communicate with the right department to make sure everyone is aware. For most cases, these changes are planned in advance and everyone is kept in the loop. Other times, you'll be thrown a curve ball and have to think about what to do on the fly.

For instance, the software you are running in a live course suddenly goes down. You are made aware of it when tickets start to come in for customer support, students are calling their academic advisors and creating discussion board posts asking about what to do. Something like this can happen and has happened to me before. Since you are the glue that holds everything together, you are responsible for communicating to all of the right stakeholders and making a backup plan and creating a backup plan for the backup plan. This scenario is more of an emergency plan, but more common changes are being assigned to work with a new SME, having due dates changed, etc. Just know that change can be around the corner.

3. Being the "Middleman"

No one likes feeling stuck in the middle. Maybe you've encountered this before with two close friends arguing or trying to stop a lovers' quarrel. Simply put, it's not fun and it's a delicate process to make sure both sides come to an agreement. Then you pray that this argument never comes up again. One part of my job that I was not prepared for was how many times I was going to be thrown into this type of situation. As the instructional designer, you're the representative of the institution. You follow the organization's guidelines, policies, and procedures. At the end of the day, you may have the final say on an important decision. Now, imagine having two other parties both believing that they are doing what's right for the organization and don't want to back down. Who is going to facilitate this conversation to make both parties see one another's views? Hint: it could be you.

I've found myself in these situations where my senior-level leadership has a disagreement with a professor, a dean, a SME, or a vendor, and I'm there to pick up the pieces and make them whole again. The tricky part of this situation is that both sides usually have the right idea in mind. They are doing what's best for the learning experience (in their opinion) and don't want to give in to the other side. This greatly depends upon your organization and the structure of your departments, but no matter the organization, these experiences can happen.

Let's say that you are developing a new Business Administration course. You are working with a professor as your SME who has taught this course for 20 years on campus. They have seen first-hand the benefits of using one particular simulation and feel that in order to achieve the same results as the in-person course, the new online course you are developing must have the same simulation. You tried out the simulation for yourself and concur that it would be a valuable tool for students. After working with the vendor, they give you a price of $50 per student and the professor confirms that the price tag is reasonable. You bring this back to your supervisor and they have several concerns about the price and mention that this would increase the cost of the course. They ask if there are alternatives that are less expensive, but still deliver the same learning experience. You then go back to your SME with this information, and they say no, it has to be this simulation or else they don't want their name associated with the course.

Is this an extreme circumstance? Yes. Did this actually happen to me in a similar situation? Yes. I constantly talk about negotiating, persuading, influencing, and handling conflict because of these scenarios. Both parties were doing what's right for the student; they wanted the best simulation and the most affordable price, but there had to be a compromise. Luckily, I did find common ground between the parties, but it took a monumental level of effort with including additional services and negotiating with the vendor.

In Between

That's Not in my Job Description?

I would like to consider this last bullet point a pro, but I also see how it could be perceived as a con. I'll let you decide though, as every instructional designer will tell you about this final point. As you continue to grow in your career, more opportunities present themselves. Sometimes, these are obvious signs for you take advantage of the opportunity, as it closely relates to your work and passions. Other times, it's outside of your comfort zone and you assume that there has to be someone else more fitting for the job. Then you realize, you are technically the most qualified to handle the task.

In order for instructional designers to make the career transition from ID to Senior ID or Manager, more responsibilities will be asked of you. If you are looking to advance to a more senior level role or leadership, it's a natural transition. The con about all of this is that this doesn't mean that anything else comes off your plate. You just continue to stack more work on top of your existing duties.

If you are working in academia, this sounds all too familiar. What's a nice change of pace, though, is being asked to conduct research, present a white paper on it, and having it be reviewed for publication. This typically is followed by presentations at conferences or being invited to speak at universities and other organizations. With every paper and presentation, you are building your brand and credibility. What about beyond this, though? That's where things start to get interesting.

When I first started working at MIT, I volunteered to run the webinars with our faculty. These webinars could be to support our students or to talk to potential students about our programs. Since I designed the courses with these faculty, it only made sense for me to host these webinars. What I wasn't expecting was that after doing this for a bit, the marketing and sales team asked if I would like to do more of these opportunities. Since I love public speaking and talking about nerdy content, I didn't think much of it until one day when I was doing a presentation for a massive organization and I had a bit of an identity crisis. Is it normal for an instructional designer to be the demo guy for products? And the answer to that question is no, but my public speaking skills have opened more doors for me instead of just being behind a laptop screen. It eventually led to partnering with the sales and marketing team to work on contracts and creating proposals. By all means, none of these things are in my job description, but I've been able to essentially mold my own customized ID role. As you can tell, I consider this a pro, but for someone who only wants to focus on creating course content and that's all, this would be their nightmare.

Overall, the pros outweigh the cons. While the cons were tricky to navigate and figure out, they did make me a more effective instructional designer. Mediating conflict and managing multiple competing priorities were excellent transferrable skills. At this point in time, I thrive in changing environments, which is something that would've terrified me years ago. If you can make a career out of being creative and caring about the student learning experience, go for it.

Learning Activities

Practice:

- If you are thinking about transitioning into the instructional design field, write down your own pros and cons list from what you've heard about instructional design. What does your list tell you about moving into this field?

- Connect with a current instructional designer and ask them about their pros and cons of the field.

Reflection:

- Think a time you went above and beyond in a role. Describe the impact this had on the organization and how you could leverage this in the future.

Chapter 3

WHAT KIND OF INSTRUCTIONAL DESIGNER DO I WANT TO BE WHEN I GROW UP?

When you were a kid, were you ever asked the question, "What do you want to be when you grow up?" Well, it's time to ask yourself this question, but rephrase it to say, "What kind of instructional designer do I want to be when I grow up?" The instructional design field is rapidly growing every day and while that's fantastic, it's also confusing. Instructional designers are in every sector from higher education, corporate, non-profit, government, and free-lance. Just saying that you want to be an instructional designer is like saying that you want to be a physician, but not identifying what type of physician.

Every call I have with a new instructional designer covers this topic because the skill sets of an instructional designer working at a university could be entirely different from an ID working for a corporation. This isn't to say that one is right and one is wrong, but more of I want you to find meaning in your work and be fulfilled. For me, it's been working in higher education and knowing that I'm providing skills for my students that will transition to the real world. For you, it could be more about leading trainings and changing the workforce. It's completely your call.

To help illustrate my point, let's look at two job postings below and break down their requirements:

Higher Education Posting:

- Bachelor's degree – Preferably advanced degree
- Experience working with faculty members, graduate employees, and students
- Experience delivering training in a workshop format
- Experience creating content using principles of Universal Design for Learning (UDL)
- Experience teaching online
- Knowledge of learning theories
- Experience with Backward Design

Corporate Posting:

- BA/BS degree (preferably in a technical field)
- 2-5+ years of experience designing and developing training curriculum
- Work or educational experience with technical and/or engineering concepts
- Able to provide an eLearning portfolio or demonstrate ability to create high-quality eLearning products
- Experience with design tools used in a learning creation environment (MS PowerPoint, Adobe Photoshop/Illustrator, Adobe Captivate, Articulate Storyline, Camtasia)
- Ability to clearly and effectively communicate in both written and oral formats
- Experience with ADDIE

As you can see from these postings, there are some similarities and differences. The higher education posting is clearly looking for someone passionate about teaching and learning. They are looking for a candidate who can apply learning theories and Universal Design for Learning to their courses and preferably to have an advanced degree. They are also looking for someone who can speak the same language as their faculty to help build strong relationships and make the design process run smoothly. They also identified Backward Design or Understanding by Design as their instructional design model, which is fairly common in higher education.

Let's examine the corporate posting. This one does not require an advanced degree, but the hiring manger is seeking someone with a more technical background. This makes sense as they are identifying the target audience of the trainings to be a more technical audience with an engineering focus. They also explicitly call out particular e-learning tools and products. Finally, their instructional design model of choice is ADDIE, a regularly used model in the corporate space.

What do these postings have in common? For starters, they are both centered around learning and developing products. Knowing how to create new knowledge is the priority for both, even though they describe this in different ways. Whether this means trainings, workshops, or courses, these learning experiences will become the majority of the job, as is the case with any instructional design role. Another significant element is building relationships with stakeholders (SMEs, faculty, etc.) and being effective communicators to all parties involved in the design process. I listed relationship management as one of the roles of an ID in the last chapter for a good reason. In every job posting you'll read, there is some mention of working with others. Lastly, while they use different instructional design models (Backward Design and ADDIE), they both still use a type of guiding framework to design their products. Most hiring managers will tell you that if you know one instructional design model, even if it's a model they don't use, that's all they want. The employee can always be trained to use the model that the organization prefers. Having this prior knowledge on how to design is incredibly valuable.

Now that we've covered the job requirements, let's talk more about the differences between these paths. In two of my podcast episodes, Heidi Kirby from the BLOC Podcast and I shared our stories about what we learned from working in both sectors. It was fun to compare and contrast these topics:

- Working with SMEs (who are those SMEs and how they're different)
- Designing for the audience (students v. employees)
- Delivering the message/lecture/training
- Designing with learning outcomes in mind
- Defining how success is measured/ROI
- Creating timing of projects/due dates
- Having autonomy versus close management
- Using e-learning tools v. LMS
- Describing common project constraints
- Identifying how ID's performance is measured?

- Playing different roles as technical specialist, project manager, etc.

- Professional development opportunities

- Salary

- Tuition reimbursement v. free tuition

- Benefits

Of course, these episodes covered the experiences of only two people. You will undoubtedly hear similar stories from others if you ask about these topics and sectors, but there is certainly the chance that you'll hear an entirely new perspective. For instance, I've worked at Southern New Hampshire University, Northeastern University, and MIT. All of these organizations treated me well and were progressive thinkers in the higher education space. If I worked at a college that treated me poorly or didn't have the necessary funding to help me, my perception of the higher education space could be entirely different. The same goes for any corporate role. It all comes down to leadership, to be honest, and what you value the most. One thing I want to make clear again is that corporate and higher education aren't the only paths to take. There are many opportunities working for the government, a non-profit organization, or working for yourself through free-lance design. With corporate and higher education being the main drivers for instructional design though, I wanted to highlight them in particular.

Now that we've covered the sectors, let's talk more about titles. In the online learning space, there are many, many titles for "instructional design." The field has grown so much that other similar jobs have been absorbed into the ID bubble. This is both wonderful and confusing at the same time. To best illustrate my point, let me talk about my team at MIT. One day, our Senior Director held a meeting and asked what each of us were passionate about. She had a collection of upcoming projects for the next fiscal year on post-it notes and we were able to pick and choose what sounded interesting to us. Another colleague and I chose the learning experience design side. My other colleagues chose the administrative projects and the LMS/engineering related projects. What I found fascinating and the best way to describe my point here is that we all have the same title, yet our jobs are incredibly different. This is basically the instructional design field in a nut shell. Saying you are an instructional designer for one organization could mean something completely different in another.

To help provide more clarity with these roles, organizations have created clearer job titles to correspond with the responsibilities. For some, it's as easy as saying Instructional Designer I or II. I've also seen Junior or Senior Instructional Designer. Perhaps Assistant Director or Associate Director of Instructional Design. All of these titles still describe instructional designers, though, implying that you are still the learning expert, project manager, relationship manager, and researcher. However, it's entirely possible to make a career out of one specific skill within this instructional design universe.

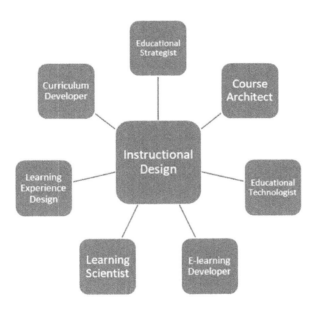

Figure 3.1: Instructional Design Paths

The figure above gives you a bit more insight into how these roles have formed, but all stem from the term "instructional design." I also didn't include related fields that instructional designers typically work with. Think of learning engineers, UX designers, graphic designers, multimedia specialists, data scientists, and copy writers.

What's special about being involved in the instructional design field now is that you have options to go down these different paths. For instance, if you love learning, and want to make a career out of how we learn, you have the option of becoming a learning scientist or learning engineer. There are entire degree programs out there for just nerding out about the learning process! If your passion is more on the technology side, you could spend hours upon hours learning about fun new tools and how to make the learning experience modern and enjoyable. For many of my colleagues, they were instructional designers first and then went into a more specific field to follow their passion.

I would be remiss not to mention those of you who have been reading this chapter and saying, "But Luke, I literally do all of these jobs!" My friend, I hear you. This is my world. Even though my current title is "Program Manager," which adds to a whole different level of confusion that I won't get into, I basically feel like a Super Instructional Designer. It's too bad that's not a title! I'm the learning expert, the tech wizard, the content developer, the project manager, and more. The funny thing is that I enjoy this. My day is never boring since I'm involved in so many projects and if you want to be the wearer of several hats too, maybe the good ol' fashioned instructional designer title is right for you.

▦ Learning Activities

Practice:

- Conduct a job search for "instructional designer" on LinkedIn Jobs and compare and contrast what you find. Write down their similarities and their differences. Which one do you think would give you more of a sense of purpose?

- From your research, what field best suits you as an instructional designer? Why?

Reflection:

- Think about your current skills within your position. What title best describes you?

Chapter 4

WHERE DO YOU SEE YOURSELF IN 5 YEARS?

Just reading this title probably gave a few of you flashbacks to a cringe-worthy interview. This question to me is straight up pain. "Let me take out my crystal ball I've been magically saving in my desk and tell you about my future." Putting my sarcasm aside, there is value in a type of question like this even though it should be reworded to say, "What are your long-term career goals and objectives?" The interviewers are looking to see if you are going to be a good fit within the organization for years to come. Think of their internal monolog as, "If I'm going to invest my time, energy, and effort into this person, are they going to stick around? Are they going to be fulfilled in this role? Will they pass along their knowledge to others? Will they make our culture better? Am I potentially making a future leader here to help retain talent?"

This is a good moment to reflect and think why you want to work at an organization. Besides a stable job and paycheck, why do you want to work for an organization for a long period of time? Do you see this organization having massive, continued success in the future? Are there multiple positions within the instructional design field that you could grow into? Does leadership seem to be bold and willing to invest in their employees? You can find a significant amount of this information online by looking up mentoring programs, trainings, job titles, benefits, tuition reimbursement, and more on Glassdoor.

For instructional designers, you need to think about what you may be passionate about in the future. I can only think of a handful of instructional designers who have always been and always will be instructional designers. Most will eventually move towards leadership positions. These positions are usually divided into leading internal teams (employees) or external teams (vendors, partners, contractors). With these new responsibilities comes a flurry of new titles in online learning such as:

- Associate Director
- Assistant Director
- Senior Learning Manager
- Online Learning Manager

- Academic Director

- Associate Vice President

- Chief Learning Officer

- Executive Director

Most of these titles will then be followed by the words "instructional design, online learning, curriculum development, learning science, distance learning, e-learning, etc." There is a multitude of new job titles coming out every year all stemming from instructional design and then progressing towards leadership positions.

Since the core of our jobs involves knowing how people learn, I've been seeing more positions seeking to capitalize on these skills in a lab setting. Every major institution has a "teaching and learning lab" in some capacity. These labs focus on building partnerships and sharing best practices for teaching and learning. They are essentially the hub of learning for their respective institutions. With online learning only growing more each day, it makes sense that the instructional design role would be transferrable to these teaching and learning labs. The same can be said for talent development in organizations. Being responsible for identifying and developing the future leaders within a company shares many of the same characteristics such as critical thinking, decision making, collaboration, project management, self-awareness, and empathy.

Now, let's actually talk about how to answer the question of where you see yourself in 5 years. Let's say that you did your homework, researched the organization, and found a page on their website dedicated to employees. You noticed that they have constantly been voted for one of the top places to work for and saw on Glassdoor that their reviews were amazing. Your sample answer could look like this:

> One of the reasons why I want to work here is because of how committed the organization is to the employees. I saw that you have been voted as one of the top places to work for and all of your reviews online talk about how leadership supports and fosters an amazing culture. As someone who loves to learn and design the learning experiences of students, it seems like a great fit to allow me to grow and learn over the next five years. I'm also passionate about building relationships and training others in instructional design. I could see myself transitioning to a leadership position to help mentor others when the time is right.

This answer will certainly change depending upon your research and how much you can learn about the organization. If you know someone personally who works there, you can also share their testimony of why the love working for the organization. Overall, make it personable and be honest with yourself of where you want your career to take you.

Learning Activities

Practice:

- While it's impossible to predict the future, it's possible to try and map out a path. What types of activities do you currently enjoy in your work? Is there a career path that aligns with these activities?

- Many promotions in the instructional design field means managing projects and leading people. Could you envision yourself in a leadership position? What leadership style speaks to you?

Reflection:

- 5 years ago, did you imagine yourself working in the instructional design field? If your answer is no, what changed this trajectory to guide you on this path?

Chapter 5

HOW DO I TEACH MYSELF A NEW SKILL?

Have you ever made your New Year's resolution to lose weight and then found yourself completely defeated a few months later? I've been there too. Every single year on December 31st, I convinced myself that this was finally going to be my year. I was going to master eating right and exercising and I would impress all of my friends and family. Like clockwork, I would find myself eating a whole pizza and give up entirely on being healthy. However, in 2016, I took a different approach and I ended up losing 30 pounds of fat in about 9 months. I was honestly floored that something actually worked. No, it wasn't a radical diet, intense exercise regimen, or fat loss supplement. They key to making an everlasting change was changing my behavior.

As I started to learn more about how people learn, it was clear that learning is an experience that takes time. Instead of building on a foundation made of sand, what if I built a healthier me brick by brick? Turns out, that was the secret to a healthy lifestyle. Instead of immediately dropping all of my calories and joining a gym, I actually made a plan! I mapped out where I wanted to go and created mini milestones along the way to assess how I was feeling and then could decide to move on to the next step. A rough example of what this looked like was:

Month 1 – Learn how to perform exercises correctly

Month 2 – Increase the weights on all of the exercises

Month 3 – Monitor and track my progress with a workout log

Month 4 – Learn how to cook using healthy recipes

Month 5 – Increase my protein intake to the correct level

Month 6 – Monitor and track my calories to make sure I'm eating the right amount

Month 7 – Work with a coach to learn more about exercise science

Every week, I would mentally check in with myself to evaluate my goals. Was I inching closer towards them? Were there any pitfalls I encountered that I could learn from to prepare a plan for next time I face them? Were there any slight changes to make to keep me on track? With each week that passed by, it became easier and easier. The main idea that I learned from this entire process was that it was challenging. There were no shortcuts and I can see how people are persuaded to buy products and misleading promises of hope. At the end of the day, though, I was able to achieve my health and fitness goals.

So, what does this have to do with instructional design? People are treating educating themselves on instructional design just like a New Year's resolution to get fit fast. You can't learn instructional design overnight. You can't learn books through osmosis. I wish it was possible, but it's not. I'm also guilty of signing up for online courses, buying books, attending webinars, participating in workshops, and more just to walk away wondering what on earth I'm going to do with this information. If you don't apply these teachings, you'll lose them. All of those tools are fantastic, but there needs to be a plan in place.

There is a right way and a wrong way with creating a plan. The "plan" I seem to hear the most is that aspiring instructional designers are going to educate themselves with every resource imaginable until they land a job. Then, the next step is to hope that their new organization has an incredible supervisor who's going to teach them the world of instructional design. Unfortunately, this isn't really a plan. There is no guarantee that your new supervisor is going to be a grand master of ID. In some cases, it's entirely the opposite problem where they don't know anything about instructional design and that's why they hired you to help. In other cases, the supervisor may have a different philosophy on learning that you don't agree with, so you'll never see eye-to-eye.

This can be a career trap if you aren't decisive. I think about this almost in a sense of competency-based education (CBE). I'd rather assess a student's knowledge by how much they know, rather than assessing by the time they spent in a classroom. You can be an instructional designer for 5 years and still only know the basics because your role never pushed you to grow. It's a common sight in the ID industry. Employees can become comfortable with their roles and the organization doesn't ask them to do more.

Without realizing it, I've accomplished all of my goals through an instructional design model known as Backward Design. This model was created by Wiggins and McTighe (2005) from their book, *Understanding by Design*, which I encourage you to purchase. Wiggins and McTighe (2005) presented an interesting perspective on how educators focused on teaching rather than learning. Think of someone struggling to learn a new skill and their solution is always to attend another webinar or purchase another book. The content is useful, but without practicing, applying, and evaluating the progress of the skill, learning doesn't take place. This process is surface-level learning of basic concepts, but it never moves beyond this point.

Here's my strategy on how to actually teach yourself a new skill. First, let's go back to the New Year's resolution of being healthier. Imagine if being healthier was a course. You would need to create learning outcomes to show what the specific goals and takeaways are for the course. These could be goals like explaining the differences between healthy foods vs junk foods, designing a healthy meal plan, producing a new healthy recipe, etc. From these outcomes, you could decide what you need to see to prove to yourself that learning is taking place. Finally, you would create opportunities to practice these skills and learn more about the basics. Below is a simplified version of this process:

Figure 5.1: Backward Design Process

For instance, let's say my outcome is to create a healthy meal from scratch. I can prove to myself that I'm learning how to do this when I don't need to follow a recipe, the dish tastes good, and it's low in calories. I would practice this skill by experimenting with different kinds of herbs and spices instead of using sugar. Finally, I would introduce myself to the basics through YouTube tutorials and cook books. Each part in this process has clear steps to show that learning is taking place. By watching YouTube videos and reading cook books, I'm starting to understand the basics of new ingredients and cooking techniques. By experimenting with different kinds of herbs and spices and then tasting them, I'm giving myself real time feedback on whether or not the dish is acceptable to my palette. I know that I'm getting better at the skill when I'm able to draw from memory what is the correct amount of ingredients for a recipe and know how to execute these actions. Lastly, I know the goal is achieved when the dish tastes great and a new sense of self-satisfaction takes over.

Now, take this concept and apply it to upskilling your abilities. For instance, your goal is to learn about Universal Design for Learning (UDL) because all of the job postings you keep applying for say that this is their preferred framework. You know that in an interview, the interviewers are going to be asking you how to apply UDL to a new course being designed or to update an existing course. This is actually becoming more and more common among instructional design interviews. So, here's how to map this out:

Outcome: Be able to apply UDL principles to an existing course

Evidence of Learning: When you are able to speak eloquently about ideas that would benefit all learners and defend your reasoning

Practice Activities: Discussing with other instructional designers about how they applied UDL to their courses and revisiting a course you previously taught or enrolled in and made updates that would benefit all students

Content: Reading Dr. Novak and Dr. Tucker's latest book on UDL and Blended Learning. Watching CAST's YouTube videos on UDL guidelines

If we put this into a chart, it would look like this:

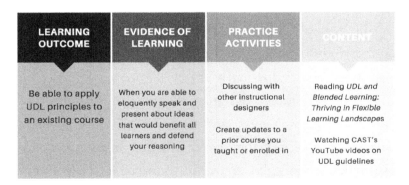

LEARNING OUTCOME	EVIDENCE OF LEARNING	PRACTICE ACTIVITIES	CONTENT
Be able to apply UDL principles to an existing course	When you are able to eloquently speak and present about ideas that would benefit all learners and defend your reasoning	Discussing with other instructional designers Create updates to a prior course you taught or enrolled in	Reading *UDL and Blended Learning: Thriving in Flexible Learning Landscapes* Watching CAST's YouTube videos on UDL guidelines

Figure 5.2: Applied Template

When it comes to teaching myself a new skill, this has been my favorite method. By breaking down the goal into smaller and smaller steps, they seem more obtainable and real to accomplish. If the outcome is to speak to applying UDL into a course, logically, you would need to be able to defend your reasoning for the changes if someone asked you why you were prioritizing one change over another. To be able to defend your reasoning, you would want to listen to what other instructional designers have gone through and what they found to be the main benefits of UDL. By practicing speaking with others, you are essentially preparing for the interview. You would also want to practice suggesting how these changes could be used in an online course. Finally, you would want to be able to learn from experts on UDL like Dr. Novak and Dr. Tucker or from the folks at CAST. By following each step and aligning them to the outcome, you'll never steer off of the path.

There needs to be a cutoff point with content to say that you are ready to move on to practicing and then move on to applying and evaluating your development. I know of far too many instructional designers who have a goal and they believe that reading more and more books will help them achieve this goal, but they never practice or take a chance with making a mistake. You need to learn from experience and this comes through trying new activities and taking chances.

Reference:

Wiggins, G. P. & McTighe, J. (2005). Understanding by design (Expanded 2nd ed.) Association for Supervision and Curriculum Development.

Learning Activities

Practice:

- Think of a valuable skill you would like to learn. Create an outline with an appropriate timeframe and relevant goals. What would be the main learning outcome? How could you assess your progress? What activities would help you practice building the skill and exploring content?

Reflection:

- What was one New Year's resolution that you didn't follow through? How would you approach this resolution differently to achieve your goal?

Chapter 6

HOW DO I BUILD A PORTFOLIO?

I was a Graphic Design major in college and a part of my required coursework was to create a portfolio that was both web-based and a physical book. Yes, back in the day, you would drive to Staples and go to their print lab with a thumb drive and pray that everything printed out the way you wanted it to. Sure enough, there were always problems. Sometimes the color didn't look quite right, an image was cut off, or the paper stock you chose was evidently the worst one possible. Luckily for all of us, we have moved away from physical copies and can now create a beautiful portfolio in a few hours. Before we cover building a portfolio though, we need to talk about a crucial component: their purpose.

The concept of portfolios in instructional design land seems to be misunderstood from the amount of conversations I've had around them.

Some aspiring instructional designers, and even current instructional designers, have never thought about creating one before. I can tell that this has been a bewildering process for those who try to apply for ID roles and dread seeing that the employer was looking to view their portfolio. The truth is that needing a portfolio isn't a new idea. In just about any kind of role, it's valuable to demonstrate your accomplishments and be able to walk someone through the process. You should be able to explain each step, the rationale, and how it all came together. This not only shows your value to an employer by seeing the final product, but arguably, it's more important to be able to express your thoughts articulately.

To help you visualize all of these steps, I'm going to provide examples for designing a new leadership program. I've somehow found myself designing and teaching several leadership courses over the years, so this is not speaking to one program in particular.

These steps were written for someone who has designed some kind of training, course, or program before. However, if you have never designed a product before, fear not! There are a few strategies you can take from this kind of project. The first is to volunteer your time to gain experience. There are many local organizations near you that would love your assistance with trying to create a product for them. I've known designers who started off creating a project for a small local business, a church, a youth group, etc. If you are looking for paid work, you could explore Fiverr or Upwork.

These do come with their own challenges, however, such as working with indecisive clients, competition and low rates. You can also make your own course. If you have a particular skill that you are passionate about with teaching others, you can always be your own SME. Lastly, many universities have had to transform their face-to-face courses into online versions, especially in the past year. If you would like to practice this activity, you could go on a university's website, find the curriculum or syllabus or a course, and use this as a case study for how you would approach the challenge.

The Steps

There should be clear and definitive elements for your portfolio:

- Introduction to the Project
- Your Role on the Project
- Problem Statement
- Research (Analysis)
- Project Goals
- Design Process
- Design Principles (Learning Models)
- Learnings / Next Steps

Introduction to the Project

Think of the introduction to the project as an "about" page. Write down the overview of the project, the timeline, and the involved stakeholders. Here is an example: During the summer of 2018, I was responsible for designing, developing, and maintaining a new leadership program for XYZ university. The goal of the project was to provide learners the necessary leadership skills to make an immediate positive impact at their organizations. The areas the learners were looking to improve upon were in strategic thinking, negotiating, understanding cultural norms, and utilizing emotional intelligence.

Role on the Project

This one is self-explanatory. You should describe your role on the project and what you were responsible for. For example, my role on this project was to serve as the lead instructional designer. I was responsible for designing and developing the course materials and curriculum. Additionally, it was my responsibility to ensure that these aligned and mapped to the created outcomes, competencies, and skills.

Problem Statement

For the problem statement, describe the problem you were trying to solve and why it was significant. What value did you create by addressing this problem? Here's one for the leadership program: Today's leaders in technical fields are incredibly educated on hard skills (coding, cloud computing, data analysis, etc.), but are lacking human skills (team work, creativity, communication, empathy, etc.). The problem I solved was being able to provide a human skills approach to education in a customized way for leaders in technical spaces. The value was to increase human skills for these technical leaders to improve their teams' functionalities and morale.

Research

Research indicates to us about how to solve a problem. You typically don't just take a chance with a complex issue. For this part of your portfolio, explain how research guided the project. What did your analysis phase look like? How did this research inform your project goals? For example, several proactive steps were taken during the research phase to indicate that a new leadership program would be successful in the technical space. The research started by drawing upon data from EMSI and Burning Glass, both of which provide the latest on job market analytics. Afterwards, I conducted interviews with experts from the technical industry and academia to determine if these findings were correct. Lastly, surveys and interviews were conducted with potential learners of the program to hear what problems they were facing surrounding leadership. Your research might not have as many steps, and it could be as simple as having your marketing team suggest the program or hearing from the dean that this was the direction your team was going to move towards. Whatever the case, there is usually a bit of behind the scenes research for creating these decisions. Do your best with describing how the analysis was guided.

Project Goals

While the main goal of the project is always to complete it on time and within budget, this section of your portfolio should specify a bit more about the behind the scenes of the design process. This is an ideal section to also use quantifiable stats. For instance, the goals of the project were to:

- Create a course to generate X amount of revenue

- Achieve X percentage using a Net Promoter Score (NPS)

- Change the behavior of X amount of employees who completed the course in an organization

- Improve student enrollment numbers, satisfaction, and retention

Design Process

Now comes the fun part! Describe how you designed the course, training, program, etc. What framework did you use to create the end product? Some of the common instructional design models are <u>ADDIE</u>, <u>UBD</u>, and <u>SAM</u>. If you have a more technical background, you might be more well-versed in Agile, Waterfall, or Phase Gate. There is no right or wrong answer here. The point is for you to walk someone through step by step how you designed the product. I also guarantee that this will be an interview question for any instructional design role, so practice in speaking to this process will be incredibly beneficial!

Learning Techniques

Learning techniques go by different names, but at the core of all of them is talking about how you made the learning process effective. It's common to see institutions rely heavily on one learning technique because they whole heartedly believe in it. A few examples that come to mind are <u>Northeastern University and experiential learning</u>, <u>WGU and competency-based education</u>, and <u>Walden University and microlearning</u>. They absolutely use other learning techniques, but their research supports their courses. What type of learning technique did you use for your design? Here are a few that can be found in online courses:

- Problem-Based Learning

- Project-Based Learning

- Scenario-Based Learning

- Case Studies

- Competency-Based Education

- Gamification

- Simulations

- Team-Based Learning

- Role Play

Once you have identified them, explain how and why you applied them in the product. For instance, one of my programs utilized scenario-based learning for every course. My colleagues and I documented how and why we used SBL in a research paper, and you can read the excerpt below for reference:

> To create an effective and optimal learning experience for real-world applications, this program's curriculum was designed using a learning technique known as, "Scenario-Based Learning" [11]. Scenario-Based Learning or SBL, uses hypothetical or real-life scenarios to support active learning strategies. These were based upon the mentioned case studies throughout the program and involved learners imagining themselves in the scenario. By going through this process, learners

needed to use critical thinking and decision-making skills throughout each part of the required problem. Learners were also able to practice and apply these skills in a safe environment where learning from mistakes and sharing their experiences with other learners was encouraged. SBL was selected for this program due to the need for technical leaders to be able to apply the learned tangible skills in the workforce.

In order to create effective scenarios, these scenarios were developed by the course team visualizing themselves as being in the position of the learners. Scenarios could be practiced safely within the program's content and aided in the learning of the transferable skills. Problems were drafted based upon the program's curriculum, articles, and videos. Once the scenarios were designed, subject matter experts and faculty members were consulted for their relevancies to a technical professional. To verify their accuracy, the course team had the opportunity to speak to learners from different industries who completed a pilot run of the program. Both quantitative and qualitative methods were utilized to collect, analyze, and apply learner feedback (Hobson, Carramolino, Bagiati, Haldi, & Roy, 2019, p. 4).

Having a paragraph or two explain the learning technique will not only show your instructional design perspective, but also your research and learning science side.

■ Learnings / Next Steps

Finally, mention what you learned from the course findings and how you used this information to improve the product. There is no such thing as a finished course. There are always methods to improve the learning experience and this is why data collection is so important. For some, this could mean evaluations from surveys. For others, it could mean focus groups, individual interviews, or observations. In whichever way you collected and analyzed the data can be highlighted and then, you can explain how you improved the product with this information. To give you an example, I asked students in a survey to tell me how long they were taking on each problem. The expectation was that it was supposed to take them 30 minutes. In actuality, these problems, took them several hours. I had the opportunity to ask them follow up questions with timing, and there was confusion around how long the submission should be. It was like trying to write an essay, but I didn't explain the page length. Since this was an open submission area, I assumed students would write a paragraph. Students assumed I wanted them to write multiple pages. This information was quickly implemented to the course by adding clearer prompts, thereby solving the problem in the future runs of the course.

Authoring Tools

First, let me say that you do not need to be afraid of authoring tools. I know that this section will make some of you nervous because you have never used an authoring tool before. These tools will not make or break an instructional designer. To be clear, you aren't a graphic designer, even though some organizations may want you to go in that direction. Luckily for you, a graphic design degree is not required to do this job. As new tools keep coming out, their developers are taking out the guesswork and making them more user friendly.

Here is where things can get confusing. If your goal is to work in the corporate space and primarily focus on e-learning, you are going to be using different tools compared to IDs in higher education and vice versa. This is not an absolute rule, but you can see these differences for yourself when you review job postings for corporate America compared to looking at a job at a university. From what I have been able to gather from many conversations with friends and colleagues who love the corporate space, you will use tools such as:

- Articulate Storyline
- Adobe Captivate
- Camtasia
- Articulate Rise

If you go on LinkedIn jobs and search for instructional design positions at some of the most well-known businesses, you will see at least two of these tools per job post. One thing to keep in mind is that many employers know these terms so they'll list all of them as their preference. In actuality though, these tools are literally competitors with one another and do the same functions. It's like saying that it's important for someone to be a master in both Canvas and Blackboard even though their properties are borderline identical. I always say that if you know one LMS, you can figure out the others. Authoring tools are the same so to speak.

Luckily, learning these tools does not need to be so complicated since many companies have tutorials on their website, YouTube or even courses on LinkedIn Learning or a similar learning platform. All of these tools have their own unique purposes, but if I had to tell you to start with one over another, I would say to go look at Rise first. The reason is two-fold. For one, Rise looks fantastic. It's easy to design on, looks great on mobile, and is relatively simple to figure out on your own. The second reason is that this will build up confidence and momentum for you as you are able to finally see your own design come to life. It's certainly still worth looking at the other tools to have a well-rounded background on them, but Rise would be my first choice.

For the folks who want to work in education, you will primarily be working in a Learning Management System (LMS). That's not to say that you won't be using any of the tools I just mentioned, because that's a possibility. I have embedded Rise before in one of my online courses for a university, so it's certainly possible to have this crossover; however, your knowledge of an LMS will be asked about first. If you don't know what this term means, an LMS is a platform that will host your course and is used to develop, deliver, and track student progress. The most popular LMS today are:

- Canvas
- Blackboard
- D2L (Desire 2 Learn)
- Moodle

Just like with the other authoring tools, you can find tutorials on any of these from the organization or YouTube. Most of them have a free trial and at the time of writing this book, Canvas is offering a free version for educators. It's worth exploring this and trying to make a course that you would feel comfortable walking someone through in an interview.

The last item I want to mention with these tools, which is extremely important, is please do not purchase all of these at once! If you added the total for all of the tools and access for an LMS, we are talking about thousands of dollars. All of the tools I mentioned above have free trials that could potentially give you enough time to feel comfortable working within them and to use those creations in a portfolio. You should also ask around your current organization to see if they have licenses already for any of these tools. I've found that many organizations have these licenses essentially on standby, waiting for someone to use them. A simple email to your IT department could save you thousands. This actually happened to me where I wanted to download Adobe's full creative suite, which is what I primarily use since I do have a graphic design background. I was thinking about purchasing this, but first I figured an email to IT wouldn't hurt to ask. Sure enough, they had a spare license and now life is good. If your organization does not have this available, my final tip is to see if your professional development funds would cover this. You might be in an organization that supports your quest for new knowledge and wants to help you move from one role to an ID role. If this is the case, a strong argument could be made to have your PD funding cover the cost of a tool, training, workshop, etc. Once again, it does not hurt to ask and this exact scenario has happened for many of my colleagues in one role within a company.

Wire Framing

Wire framing is a bit underrated with a portfolio, but for designing courses, I feel that it's necessary. You are trying to demonstrate to the interviewers that you know how to create a learning experience, and putting each concept together will show this. Essentially, you are breaking down the parts of courses and showing how they would align within a module or section. For instance, you are showing what the student journey is going to look like in the course. The student's activities for the week are a reading, videos, a practice problem, and a discussion board posting. For wire framing purposes, this could look like:

Figure 6.1: Wire Framing Process

This is an incredibly simplified way of showing the learning experience. You can also expand this out to show how the learning outcomes align to the learning objectives and how these align to the assignments and content. That might be overdoing it for a portfolio, but when applying to a job in higher education, they'll love seeing this outline.

There many amazing tools out there to help you demonstrate this design process. Some other tools might make more sense for your target audience. I specifically use Google Sheets to show how my courses map out for each section when I'm working with SMEs or the marketing department.

These are folks who want to see everything, but you want to keep it simple to read, to make comments on, and to share. If you are working as a team and want to do this activity with other designers, you could use more sophisticated tools like Figma or Adobe XD. Once again though, I like Google Sheets since they are universal. Everyone knows what they are and they are easy to read.

Graphics and Video

You don't need to be a graphic designer to make something look aesthetically pleasing. Adobe Spark and Canva (not to be confused with Canvas) are both relatively easy to use. They both come with tutorial videos to help you learn about all of their features. One tool that I have used for videos before is called, "Bitable." What's nice about Bitable is that they have realism footage along with animations. You aren't stuck to one particular style and this opens up more doors for creativity. I personally don't use Vyond, but I know of plenty of designers and trainers who do. This platform is an easy way to create professional looking animations. If you have ever done a training in HR before, I bet you'll recognize Vyond. If you want to record your own type of tutorial walking students through a process, you can use Camtasia, which I mentioned already, for screen recording and editing. There is nothing wrong with recording on Zoom and editing with whatever tool your laptop comes with either!

I've actually used iMovie and Adobe Premiere for editing my own videos. With a few hours under your belt, you'll be able to zip through any of programs for designing graphics and videos.

Website

The final piece to puzzle is your website. You don't necessarily need your own website, but I do find it helpful for hosting all of your content in one location. A separate website also builds your brand awareness. Some of the aforementioned platforms additionally serve as a content provider. If you want your own website, you could use Squarespace, Wix, or Weebly. Once again, you don't need a website, but I would recommend one. I prefer Squarespace over anything else because of how customizable the designs are. My website is done through Squarespace if you want to see an example.

Reference:

Hobson, L., Carramolino ,B., Bagiati, A., Haldi, T., & Roy, A. (2020) Teaching and learning technical and managerial leadership skills through scenario-based learning. Retrieved from: https://www.sefi.be/wp-content/uploads/2020/11/Proceedings-DEF-nov-2020-kleiner.pdf

Learning Activities

Practice:

- If you haven't yet created a portfolio, connect with local organizations and volunteer your design services.

- If you have the necessary content to make a portfolio, create an outline from all of the topics in this chapter. Fill in the details to write your first rough draft. This doesn't need to be perfect, but taking this first step will help out tremendously!

Reflection:

- What is one major finding you learned about from a project?

Chapter 7

HOW DO I MAKE CONNECTIONS IN THIS FIELD?

Years ago, I received some puzzling career advice that completely changed the trajectory of my life. Back in 2016, I couldn't seem to break into the instructional design field. I was knocking on the door, but couldn't get it. At the time, I was working at a university with a perplexing title called, "Creative Resources Manager." This meant that I developed the resources and online learning communities for the academic support team for around 60,000 students. While I loved many aspects of my role, I wanted to be an ID. Something about this job title fascinated me with being able to design a student's education. I spoke with several colleagues about how they became IDs and they all gave me some wonderful advice. However, it was two conversations in particular that I couldn't get out of my head. These were from two colleagues, who I greatly respected and still do to this day, and they told me about the power of leaving my comfort zone to grow. While I always knew about this from a mental perspective of trying to increase my skill set, they meant it as physically leaving my comfortable bubble at my university to think about my career. Don't just think about the next job or next year. Think about where you want to be in 5 years and go do that now. Learn from other perspectives and take these with you on your journey.

I honestly sat there dumbfounded for the longest time and then was like, "Okay, it's time to take action. What do I do first?" Luckily for me, I decided to revise my old LinkedIn profile. I updated my bio, education, skill set, and preferences. I figured that a potential employer would probably try to find me on LinkedIn to learn more about me. What I didn't realize was just how powerful LinkedIn could be. You see, I decided to apply to jobs with a new button at the time called, "Apply with LinkedIn."

This button pulled my information and auto-populated the fields on the application, which saved quite a bit of time! What I didn't expect though was that any of my existing connections on LinkedIn would appear after I submitted the application. While scouring the LinkedIn Jobs page, I found an instructional designer job at Northeastern University. The job seemed to match my skill set and I eagerly applied with this LinkedIn button. To my amazement, a former colleague of mine at SNHU worked there and better yet, the ID role was in her department. I reached out to her to learn everything I possible could about Northeastern and what the switch was like from transitioning from one university to another. With this connection, I gained an edge and I knew I would at least have a shot at an interview. Long story short, I made a good enough impression in my interviews to be offered the job. It was at this moment that I realized the power of LinkedIn and how valuable networking truly was.

This leads into this chapter's topic: how to build a network. As I progressed in my instructional design career, it became apparent to me that I didn't know enough instructional designers. I knew my inner circle, but I didn't have a clue what other IDs were practicing or reading about. I began to crave making more relationships with other like-minded individuals and it reached a point where I told my director that one of my professional goals was to meet more IDs. By building this network I didn't realize the impact it would have on my growth from both a professional perspective, but also from a job-hunting perspective. I'm going to share with you what I've learned along the way and whether it's to help you land a job, find the right connection, build your network, or just to simply make your LinkedIn newsfeed better, I got you covered.

For years, I just accepted anyone's request and would add whoever. This always felt weird to me and I wondered why anyone would use this platform. My newsfeed was filled with things I didn't care about like politics and cat pictures. LinkedIn finally threw me a bone with recommending that I start to add other instructional designers at my university. After connecting with a few of them, the algorithm slowly introduced more IDs into my recommendations and my ID network finally had a foundation. I was baffled to see my newsfeed change from random things like politics and cat pictures to relevant topics pertaining to online learning. Blog posts, articles, podcasts, YouTube videos, and more populated every day and I found myself entrenched in so much nerdy content. I get asked how I stay up to date with trends in the instructional design field and all I need to do now, I just log into LinkedIn and see what my connections are talking about.

What if I told you the way to find a new job isn't just through a job recruiting website, but through people? Yes, as my network grew, I started to notice this recurring trend: instructional designers post instructional design opportunities. I would constantly see posts saying something like, "My team is hiring. I'm going to share the job posting as soon as it comes out. Message me for more details!" While I was surprised at first at the number of these posts, this does make a ton of sense. They are the ones who are well aware of what's happening internally and it's fairly common for the manager to spread the word before the general public knows. I've had many conversations with hiring managers trying to tap into my network to see if I know of candidates looking for specific ID roles. These conversations usually occur before the job posting is even made or released. If you make the right connections, you'll have a competitive edge.

Maybe you are like me from back in the day where you are just starting to build your ID network. Where do you find these fabulous instructional designers? My tip here is to join several ID groups on LinkedIn. If I click on my groups section, these are some of them that pop up:

- Instructional Designers in Higher Education
- Higher Education Management
- EDUCAUSE
- Instructional Design Central (IDC)
- The ID Newbies
- Data-Informed Learning Design
- eLearning Industry

I'm also a part of local groups for IDs who used to meet up in person, back when that was a thing. The IDs in these groups are here to share, learn, and grow, just like you. What you'll notice with looking at these groups too is that they are diverse. From newbie groups, to veteran IDs, to higher education in general, to corporate, and more, there is a group for every kind of ID topic and it's great to hear so many perspectives. If you are a learning nerd, I'd welcome you to join the <u>Instructional Design Institute Community</u>.

The other key part that you need to know with joining these groups is how to act in them. I feel like 2021 is going to be the year when human beings need to relearn social skills. Being in an online group doesn't mean that you have the right to spam blast your products all day every day. Imagine being in a room with 50 people and instead of starting to mingle and slowly introduce yourself to others, you picked up a megaphone and started to yell into it. That's what it feels like and chances are, you'll be muted or blocked shortly thereafter. Once again, think about those human skills that have been buried by Zoom and uncover them. Comment on posts. Ask thought provoking questions. Ask for advice. Provide helpful recommendations and tips (if you are speaking about a topic you are well versed in). Overall, be kind and show a genuine interest.

I received a message one day from someone who wanted to pursue an EdD at Northeastern University. By typing in EdD and Northeastern University in the search bar, my profile popped up. Even though my EdD is not from NU, my profile still appeared since I was an ID there and I had an EdD. We had a great chat about doctorates in general and I personally knew the team that designed NU's program so I could speak to details of the program. Later on, I actually used this same tip when it came to trying to connect with more IDs at my own institution. There really wasn't an easy way to find every single ID across all of MIT, so using the search bar and typing in "Instructional Designer MIT," I managed to pop up people I hadn't met before. I was able to network with a few of them and discuss best practices and talk more about our positions. It sounds silly, but institutions are massive. There is no easy way to meet everyone in your own school, but this tip can help you connect with the right people.

For those of you that are trying to transition from one job to another, I'd recommend using this tip and seeing if someone would have a type of virtual coffee chat with you. I love what I do and where I work, but hypothetically speaking, if I was going to try to work at a different university, I'd want to connect with someone and get a feel for the organization.

- How's the culture?
- What's leadership like?
- Do IDs have a valued say in the decision-making process?
- Do you work on a team?

Questions like these can get the conversation going and give you a sense of "is this the right place for me?" Don't just settle on any kind of ID position. Find the right one for you. I understand that trying to find a job is crazy right now, but you need to find an organization that's going to treat you with respect and will value your skillset.

Reaching Out to Individuals

Imagine you've decided to use my last tip and you want to connect to a specific person. How do you do this without being weird and awkward? Honestly, it's a good question! We've all received messages from someone on LinkedIn and decided not to respond. It's just like introducing yourself at a conference and you're nervous so you accidentally fumble over your words. The key to this is to act like a genuine person. Let's look at a real message I received before that made me feel like an actual person was trying to connect with me and not a robot:

> "Hey Luke, I hope this reaches you well (I'm sure you heard this phrase about 10 times this week!) but I hope you are. I really appreciate reading your articles and content posted about online learning and management. If you ever have the time, I would really appreciate a small 10-15 minute window of your time to connect via Zoom. As I venture into the online world of higher ed, I would love to learn from your experiences.
>
> Appreciate your time,
>
> Syeda"

This message to me said that she was a normal person with a sense of humor. I remembered her name because she commented on a few of my blog posts before in the past. I wrote back to her and we scheduled a time to talk more about higher education and online learning. We continued to chat and talk about her journey to becoming an ID and I was over the moon thrilled for her when she landed her dream job. Funny enough, she ended up becoming the first member of Instructional Design Institute and her feedback was vital to what it is today. Let's go back to her message though. She wrote to me as a genuine person coming from the stance of wanting to learn more. There was no sales pitch or hidden intention. Now keep in mind that not everyone will respond to you and that's okay. Not everyone checks LinkedIn and honestly, LinkedIn could be a full-time job if you let it. I still have unread messages in my inbox that I try to clear later on because I am swamped most days. Just remember my example about how one message turned into a new friendship.

So far, I've talked about connecting with other instructional designers. There is however value in connecting with other people in different professions like recruiters, consultants, and hiring managers. These people are purposefully seeking out the help of instructional designers. By connecting with these folks, you are seeing in real-time the latest job postings for entire organizations or sectors. Connecting with them is also helpful as a reminder of who is hiring and for what role. I've been using the term "instructional design" throughout this entire post, but there are many, many jobs that can be classified into the ID category. This will let you find the right ID fit whether this means you fall more on the learning science side or perhaps the tech side or maybe you are accustomed to doing it all.

There is one person in this field though who you need to connect with and this is <u>Eric Domke</u>. To try and help other IDs become more aware of the latest opportunities, I've been sharing new job postings that pop up on my feed. Eventually, I realized that many of these opportunities relate back to one of my connections commenting on the postings, making them appear in my feed. That connection is, as you probably guessed, Eric. Since I've connected with Eric, I've seen ID positions for Netflix, Disney, Spotify, etc. He's able to, and still not sure how he does this, track down every ID job and bring them to others attention. Give him a follow or connect with him. You can mention that I sent you over to him.

If you are able to put any of these steps in practice, your network is going to blossom. I attribute my network to this entire instructional design journey. You need the right people around you to help you grow. Build your network and see the results for yourself!

Learning Activities

Practice:

- Connect with at least one new person today. Select any of the tips above and make a new connection with someone in the instructional design field.

Reflection:

- Think about your current network. Who could you bring together to show your value as a networker? For instance, Peter Shea connected me with Dr. Kapp and now he's a part of this book!

Chapter 8

IS AN INSTRUCTIONAL DESIGN DEGREE RIGHT FOR ME?

Whether you need to go back to school for an instructional design degree is an open question. I covered this topic extensively already with the help of Tim Slade, author of *eLearning Designer's Handbook*, and Dr. Karl Kapp, Professor of Instructional Technology at Bloomsburg University. The answer to this question really comes down to your preferences, your prior education, and your goals. For this chapter, I'm going to assume that you have made your final decision and you want to go back to school for an ID degree. As someone who holds several degrees, I understand the pursuit of knowledge and the satisfaction of completing such a monumental feat. This then leaves us with the question of how to go about with applying for an instructional design degree program.

In my opinion, there are several significant steps to take before even considering what university to apply to. Do not blindly apply to degree programs. You actually hold quite a bit of power when it comes to selecting your school. You see, every institution wants you to apply to their program and they will spend thousands of dollars on ads to try and recruit you. Once you click on a link for their institution, they are capturing your data. This is known as tracking pixels. This tells their marketing department your behavior when it comes to what ads you prefer to click on, how long you stay on their advertisements, and more. This then allows them to market to you again on Facebook, LinkedIn, Twitter, and YouTube. They can decide how often to push a new ad campaign to you. The point of this is not to make you think that universities are trying to invade your life, but more that this is a strategy to make you feel more comfortable with the university, and eventually, enough reminders might convince you to apply to their program.

Instead of advertising dictating where you should go to school, I propose three strategies to that will give you the real and honest details. These three strategies are:

1. Communicating with current students and alumni

2. Researching the curriculum and outcomes

3. Connecting with professors, directors, and deans

If you are able to follow through with each of these strategies, you'll have the right answer for you.

Communicating with Current Students and Alumni

What better way to learn about the program then from the students currently experiencing it? Students within the program will give you honest feedback about what they love about the learning experience and perhaps what they would like to see changed. No institution is perfect and we have all had a fair share of times when we were excited to take a course because of the way the course description was written, only to find out that the course didn't live up to expectations. I can think of a few courses I've taken where the course description outlined the most incredible course, only to have the professor skip elements of the course or not be that passionate about the material. Ask current students about their experiences, what they love about the courses, what they want to see changed, what the professors teaching style was like, how the program was going to equip them with real world skills, etc. Your conversations with them can also be quite revealing. For instance, if someone is close to graduating, but they express frustration over the program having an overly narrow focus when it comes to career preparation, that's a major sign to avoid the program.

You should also absolutely connect with alumni of the program. Where are they now? What have they accomplished? Would they recommend the same program to you? Speaking with alumni might be the most important step here. If you talk to an alum and they speak about the program with pride and appreciate how it has led to them securing their dream job, then all signs point to yes, you should apply there. If they say that all they learned about were learning theories and don't know how to create a portfolio, run away.

It's actually relatively easy to find these people as well. LinkedIn, Facebook, or Twitter are going to be your go-to sources. Facebook groups are specifically helpful when it comes to connecting with students and alumni. I've seen it happen hundreds of times where someone makes a post in an instructional design group saying, "I'm considering applying to XYZ university. Can someone share with me their experiences about the ID program?" It's a quick and easy way to make new connections and find out the truth. There are also dedicated alumni groups that are typically on Facebook and LinkedIn.

Researching the Curriculum and Outcomes

I alluded to this point already, but let me drive this home. There are some poorly designed instructional design degree programs out there. This is also incredibly ironic given that instructional designers create the courses that compose the degrees, but I digress. You must thoroughly research what the program is going to cover. Dig through all of the pages on the curriculum, the course outcomes, the course descriptions, and more. Do not assume that the institution is going to cover all of your needs. I made this fatal error years ago when it came to pursuing a degree in graphic design. I didn't realize what I had gotten myself into until my junior year, when I realized that the courses were missing extremely important topics for the real world. You know who had to take multiple courses on Flash? This guy. You know what program died a few months later and became obsolete? Flash. The year I was graduating was also the year that custom website builders like Wix/Squarespace were launched. Literally the writing was on the wall that I was not prepared for the real world and it was too late. You know what could have prevented this? If I had thoroughly researched all of the design courses and talked to alumni to ask them about what skills they had to teach themselves once they finished their schooling. I ended up doing this too late and a majority of my friends who were in the same program did not become graphic designers. Please do not let this happen to you.

What should you look for in a program? You should be looking for these topics:

- Online Course Design
- Learning Sciences
- Instructional Design Models
- Learning Theories
- Learning Analytics
- Learning Techniques
- Authoring Tools / Web Development
- LMS Administration
- Working with SMEs
- Managing Projects
- Leading Teams
- Research (Quan/Qual/Mixed)
- Blended Learning
- AR/VR
- Gamification
- Evaluating Learning
- Building a Portfolio
- Internships

As you can see from this list above, there are a decent number of topics involving learning. Knowing how people learn is the most significant part of your job. From there, people skills are equally as important. Next, comes the necessary technology with tools, the web, LMS knowledge, etc. You are also going to need experience, which you can gain from internships and designing a portfolio with hopefully some kind of volunteer project, free-lance work, etc.

Unfortunately, I've heard horror stories where instructional design students will only learn about learning theories and that's it. While that's clearly integral to the ID role, I'd argue that managing relationships is the most challenging part of the job. If you don't know how to influence, negotiate, or persuade stakeholders on key decisions, your ideas will fall flat. You need the well-balanced approach of each element to be successful.

Connecting with Professors, Directors, and Deans

As I mentioned before, you, as a potential student, hold the power to be able to decide where you want to go back to school. You have the ability to connect with professors, faculty members, program directors, deans, teaching assistants, and others who work for the institution. These people should be thrilled that you want to chat more about the program and they should be proud to tell you more about it. It's an opportunity to showcase what they've accomplished and how they can help you too.

Learning from my past mistakes with my bachelor's degree, I decided to do all of these steps when I considered applying for a doctorate. One of my graduate professors mentioned that SNHU had a relatively new EdD program and it sounded like it was exactly what I was looking for. Before I got ahead of myself, I researched who was responsible for the program and found their email on SNHU's website. I emailed the director at the time, Dr. Peg Ford, and told her about my ambitions and what I was looking for in a doctoral program. I sent over a few questions and anxiously awaited her reply. I received an email the next day with an invitation to come and shadow two course sessions and then to chat with her in person. I'll never forget this kind gesture and right from the start, I could tell how much she believed in the EdD program. I took her up on this offer and planned a trip to campus for a fun filled Saturday of doctoral classes. While I was observing them, I could tell how much passion the students and professors had. It was unlike any kind of class I had experienced before. After that day, I was convinced that this was the program for me. I'm not expecting everyone to do this, but anyone who is willing to go out of their way and give you phenomenal customer service means you should be paying attention.

You can find these faculty members and employees on the university's website or on LinkedIn. Complete the same practice when reaching out to students and alumni. Ask them what makes their program amazing and stand out from the others. Ask about the work their students have completed and about their journeys.

Finally, I want to give one last piece of advice. If you apply and are accepted into your ideal ID program, you need to go above and beyond. Your courses won't cover every topic because you'll always be a life-long learner and the field is constantly changing. When you have enough ambition and foresight to think about what other ways of learning you could pair with your education, you'll truly develop as a designer. I clearly didn't do things correctly when I went for my bachelor's. What's funny, though, is that I have a real-life example of the "what could've been." Someone very close to me pursued the same graphic design degree around the same time as me. She realized that her courses weren't going to equip her with all of the necessary skills for the job and she began to take courses on LinkedIn Learning and Code Academy. She read books on the future of UX and UI when these terms weren't commonly known. Instead of being afraid of change, she went all in. She now leads a team of UX designers for Wayfair and is one of the hardest working people I've ever met. This person is my wife, by the way, and I know that if you can replicate what she did, you'll be a rockstar.

Learning Activities

Practice:

- After you find the ID degree you want to pursue, connect with at least 2 current students and 2 alumni. Interview them about their experiences with the program.

- Connect with one of the faculty members from the program on LinkedIn or by email. Ask them about how and why their program can help you in instructional design.

Reflection:

- Think back to a recent course you enjoyed. What was it about that class that you want to find in another course?

HOW DO I OBLITERATE IMPOSTER SYNDROME?

Chapter 9

If you have ever uttered the words: "why would they listen to me?" "am I qualified enough for this?" "I'm nothing special," or anything remotely close, this chapter is for you. Imposter syndrome is ugly. When doubt grabs ahold of you and makes you feel insignificant, it's a hurtful experience. There are no other ways to describe it. Sometimes, it takes an outside perspective to help make this feeling disappear, and hey, I'm here to help you with that! What do I know about imposter syndrome? Well, for starters, do you think someone who struggled with learning would make a good instructional designer? Probably not and I thought the same thing about myself.

First, let me tell you about my experience with this. I never called this experience by these words and imagine my surprise when I began to read more about this years later on LinkedIn. I thought I was the only one who secretly felt like a fraud. One day, I finally had enough courage to confide in someone with how I felt and I gave an example of someone I looked up to in higher education. I sang his praises and talked about how he was clearly the top expert in online learning and I wasn't sure if I could ever reach his level of success. Then, I was given some simple advice that blew my mind: "Why don't you go talk to him about your goals?"

"Are you serious," I thought to myself. He must be the busiest man on the planet. He has no idea who I am and there is no way he would speak to me.

Turns out, I was wrong. He welcomed the chance to talk to someone about their career within higher education. As I sat in his office listening to him talk, I could see my friends walking by and wondering what on earth the meeting was about. As we were chatting, I began to slowly piece together that my perception of him was wrong. He wasn't born a genius. He wasn't given a magical golden ticket to become the expert in online learning. Instead, he had a thirst for knowledge that couldn't be quenched. He went back to school several times after his PhD because he wanted to be in the classroom and learn more. He was a lifelong learner. That's when I noticed that almost everyone I looked up to in the higher education space got to where they were through hard work, determination, and grit. Did these same people ever feel like imposters too? Most likely, yes. Maybe this changed when they had the proper job title that demanded respect or they were sought out because of their publications or research. Whatever the case, I learned a valuable lesson in that everyone has to start somewhere.

Now, I'm going to reveal to you my secret of how to obliterate imposter syndrome and by doing this, you'll also increase your value to an employer. The secret is... to build your brand. You want to carve out your own niche of becoming the "go to" person for the topic. Even if there are other educators already in this space, that's okay! You can provide your own unique perspective and further develop an idea. It's never too late to build your brand.

One of my favorite stories about building a brand and turning it into an empire is the story of how one person made fantasy football mainstream. There are an estimated 60 million people who play fantasy football each year and the industry is worth around $7.2 billion dollars (Willingham, 2020). If you've never played fantasy football before, all you need to know is that the premise is creating your own dream team of players and competing against your friends and family. It's a rather silly concept where kids and adults become extremely passionate about make believe points for a game that isn't real; however, it's captivated millions of people. It was all started by a man named Matthew Berry, the writer for the movie *Crocodile Dundee* and the sitcom *Married... with Children*.

The person who solely created this phenomenon by bringing it to ESPN and other media giants actually had imposter syndrome! I listened to an interview of his before and the host asked him if he could've predicted this explosion in fantasy sports. His response was, "No, I didn't think anyone would listen to me." I'm sure plenty of people didn't listen to him. After all, what does a sitcom writer know about sports? But the more his audience grew, the more influence he had. The more influence he had, the more opportunities appeared. Repeat these same steps enough, and there you go. He didn't try to become a football player. He didn't go into coaching. He didn't try to become a commentator. He simply stuck with one area and never looked back.

The best educators that you know of aren't masters of everything. They are incredibly intelligent in one area and then explored others. Think of some of the major people in our field. What are they known for?

Here are a few below:

- Dr. Karl Kapp – Gamification
- Julie Dirksen – Design for How People Learn
- Connie Malamed – the eLearning Coach
- Dr. Katie Novak – Universal Design for Learning
- Ant Pugh – eLearning Freelance

I replicated the patterns of the highly successful educators above. Back in 2016, you probably had no idea I existed. I was working the typical 9-5 and didn't explore networking or professional development opportunities. I didn't want to speak out. I didn't want the spotlight. Slowly, but surely, it started to happen. I became obsessed with creating online learning communities and started to give talks around the university to academic advisors, students, and faculty. I still struggled with the fact that my own university didn't believe in me enough to give me a chance on the role I wanted and it was strange to see the people every day in the hallways who denied me the instructional design positions. With every rejection letter, I worked harder and harder and finally found better opportunities elsewhere.

I will say that imposter syndrome can sneak back up every now and again, even if you don't think about it. I was invited to give a presentation on working with SMEs for a well-known university after the director of their online programs saw one of my YouTube videos. I was flattered by the invitation to speak at one of the most innovative universities in the online space. I asked the audience how long they had been in instructional design as I figured there would be a mix of newbies and veterans in the crowd. I was baffled when the chat box kept filling with replies of numbers like 20 years of experience, 25 years of experience, and more. There was actually one person attending my talk who had been an instructional designer for longer than I've been alive! Imposter syndrome hit me like a brick wall as my mind started to race with thoughts about, "Why is someone with 25 years of experience being an ID listening to my talk?!" After a few deep breaths, I remembered about how even I go to talks on a topic I'm familiar with, but I'm curious on learning another perspective. Eventually, imposter syndrome faded away as I found my rhythm with the talk and was met with applause at the end.

My advice for you is to pick one topic you are passionate about and become immersed in it. Let's say you love learning about UDL. What can you do? You can download podcasts on UDL, you can buy books, you can take courses online, you can watch YouTube videos, you can watch TED Talks, and more. UDL should be all that you think about. Eventually, you can practice what you learned and apply them to your courses. Interview others to hear about their experiences and talk to the students and faculty about your implementations. Build a network around what you are passionate about and find likeminded people. Start talking about your ideas with them. It's one thing to be able to write about your ideas; it's another to speak to them coherently. The invitations, the titles, the jobs, and all of the accolades will come. You just need to start. Over time, your confidence will sky rocket and you'll be amazed at how far you can go.

Learning Activities

Practice:

- Think of an area you want to further develop and that you are self-conscious about. What could you do to reduce this feeling? Describe your plan on how you'll become immersed in the subject.

Reflection:

- Reflect back to a time you felt imposter syndrome. What triggered this occurrence? How could you get around this obstacle in the future?

Chapter 10

HOW DOES PUBLIC SPEAKING IMPACT MY CAREER?

I was introduced to public speaking at an early age. I personally didn't start practicing this skill until I was in college, but I was exposed to it as a child without realizing it. Growing up, my father was a deacon in our church. For those of you who didn't grow up Catholic, think of a deacon as a preacher with extra responsibilities. Every Sunday, my dad would approach the pulpit and deliver a sermon. At first, I didn't give it a second thought. I've always thought my dad was incredible, so it made sense to me that he would go up and speak in front of hundreds of people. After a while, though, I noticed that more and more people began to show up in church that I had never seen before. I stopped focusing on my dad when he was speaking and I started to notice how these parishioners were hanging on his every word. After mass, it was impossible to approach him as there was a massive line of churchgoers wanting to talk to him. It felt like I was at a concert and I was cutting all of the fans in line eagerly waiting for their rock star's autograph. Little did I know the impact this would have on my adult life.

I still remember the day when I decided to try and replicate my dad's presence. I was in a Marketing course at Southern New Hampshire University and my professor was laser focused on preparing us for the real world. Her experience taught her about the importance of public speaking with winning over clients and closing deals, so the course content revolved around replicating these experiences. The assignment was to create a persuasive speech. I was fortunate enough to present towards the end of the class and was able to witness other students not being fully prepared for the blunt criticism that was launched at them. I was determined not to make the same mistakes as my peers, and I prepared for this presentation like my life depended on it. I took what I remembered from how my dad prepared for his sermons and applied them to my methods. The day of the presentation came and I gave it literally everything I had. While I was presenting, I remember thinking, "what on earth am I doing? No one tried this hard before you and you are going to look like a fool at the end of this." I finished the presentation, said thank you, and then waited. I heard silence. I stood there sweating bullets, fearing I just royally screwed up. After what felt like an eternity, I heard a sound, and it was my friend sitting in the front row as he uttered the word, "Wow." After that, I was hooked on public speaking.

For me, public speaking means influence. It means leadership. When you think of critical skills for instructional designers, public speaking is never mentioned. I can promise you that public speaking won't be a qualification or a preference on any job posting. Why would someone focused on designing learning experiences need to master the art of talking in front of others? Well, there are several reasons:

- Giving demos and walkthroughs of courses
- Presenting at conferences
- Delivering workshops
- Hosting webinars
- Hosting trainings for faculty
- Winning over SMEs
- Acing interviews
- Recording podcasts

While a portion of my role is on designing the courses and all the normal instructional design responsibilities, there is a tremendous percentage of my job where there is a microphone in front of my face. There is going to come a point in your life as an instructional designer where you are going to have to speak about your projects and sell the audience on your accomplishments. This could mean success rates, enrollment numbers, retention efforts, number of courses designed, positive feedback, incorporating new learning strategies, using learning analytics, and other initiatives. The most significant component of whatever you are speaking about is the delivery of the message.

Most people hate public speaking and if you can make this skill become your super power, you'll increase your value in your organization. So, how do you become a great public speaker? Here is my condensed advice:

1. Get Comfortable with Being Uncomfortable

If you have never practiced public speaking before, this is going to feel awkward, incredibly awkward, but that's okay! It means you're growing and you're honing a new skill. I guarantee that your favorite speakers have spent hours upon hours practicing their lines. Before you dive into anything, you need to have the right mindset around this process. Think of this as an exciting endeavor where your future is completely in your hands.

2. Find a Style and Emulate It

Who inspires you? What speech resonated with you, where the words were buzzing inside of your head and you couldn't stop thinking about it? That's the person you should emulate. The beauty of this exercise is that you can learn about how people speak and find the one that's relatable. There isn't a correct style. For me, it was clearly my dad and I replicated his style. I noticed that he paused at dramatic moments and then sped up to build the suspense. His volume would gradually increase as the speech progressed and then he brought it back down at the right levels to provide emphasis on particular parts.

I never ruled out the styles of other amazing public speakers. Another favorite of mine is actually the fitness trainer, Tony Horton, who created the P90X workout DVDs (yes, those old things in your closet). Did you know he's an incredible public speaker too? He is a comedic story teller and adds in so much detail about every scenario that you can envision it as if you were there. His rags-to-riches story is inspiring on many levels, from personal development to improving overall health and wellness. Every time I hear one of his speeches, I immediately think about my next workout. Go out and find these kinds of speakers who inspire you.

3. Script It Out

Some people out there have the gift of "winging it." That's when you don't prepare at all and somehow can deliver a powerful speech. I absolutely can't do this. Most professional speakers need to put pen to paper to have the words come out right. You don't need to physically write out your entire speech, but having an outline or a loose script will certainly help you. It's also much more efficient to remember the content in pieces. For instance, when I'm giving a speech, I'll script out the bullet points for each slide and then speak to the slides. This allows me to fill in the gaps. It reminds me of having an open book test where I'm still trying to remember the information on my own, but I have a little bit of help.

4. Practice

This is my secret. It's an obvious secret. In order to become great at a skill, you must practice. My secret is that I actually follow through and practice. I'll rehearse the same speech 3-4 times a day leading up to the event. It has always been something I've been self-conscience of because my family has always listened to me talk to myself in my office for hours. Eventually, I got over this feeling because I could see noticeable changes in how I present after practicing. This was a tip I picked up from my dad. During the week, he would practice his speeches as if there were a live audience in our basement listening to his words. I began to notice little things great public speakers do like inflection, pausing, tempo changes, and more. It's like he was writing a song that he knew the audience would never be able to get out of their heads. You need to experiment with this because it's so unusual at first. It's not normal to raise your voice and wait for an audience's reactions. Overtime, though, your practicing will create your own style.

5. Record Yourself, Scrutinize, and Apply Feedback

How do you become great at public speaking? I don't mean good. I mean great. The answer is to record yourself and find ways to improve. Recording your own speeches takes time to do and you need to be vulnerable to watch the playback. Whatever is on the video is going to be the honest truth and sometimes, that's a lot to handle. The most common noticeable part of your speech will be "filler" words. These are the words you say when you are trying to transition from one thought to another. These could include, you know, uh, um, like, and so on. It takes practice to remove these from your vernacular. Also, be aware of your body language. Does it read as being disengaged, intense, uninterested, or anything else that could make the audience uncomfortable?

Once the plans are in place and you follow these steps, you'll be on your way to being a great public speaker.

Learning Activities

Practice:

- Create a 5 – 10-minute speech on the benefits of your favorite topic. Complete a few practice runs and then record your speech. Identify areas that you would make your presentation sound more convincing.

Reflection:

- Think about your favorite presentation or speaker. What did you feel during the talk? What was it about the speaker that you found so engaging?

Chapter 11

HOW DO I NAVIGATE BETWEEN DIFFERENT CULTURES AT WORK?

As I've mentioned before, human skills, people skills, soft skills, or whatever you want to call them, matter. They are essential to an instructional designer. If you can't work with others, you are dead in the water. Over the years, I noticed how many individuals identify with an organization's culture (beliefs, values, and behaviors). There were always outliers in the culture, though, and I couldn't put my finger on how these were different. For instance, within a university, the employees believe in a certain culture and identify with it. However, they also believe in the culture of their school, their department, and their team. These are called "subcultures," and they are essential to understand when trying to manage a project and your career growth.

As I progressed in my career as an academic advisor, instructor, instructional designer, and program manager, it was a revelation to learn how each position held its own subculture, despite having the same organizational culture. When an organization does well, this growth drives the organization's culture and subcultures to change. I witnessed this first hand while working at one university. My original team of 12 grew to 24, and then 50, and then even more. This growth created the need for smaller teams with new leaders taking charge and existing team members being reassigned to new teams to help with training new employees. In essence, each team had their own subculture, even though we were all under the same organizational umbrella.

All of my experiences actually made sense according to the cultural research of MIT Professor Ed Schein. Schein (2017) mentioned how, "Organizational success usually produces the need to grow; with growth and aging, organizations need to differentiate themselves into functional, geographic, product, market, or hierarchical units" (p. 229). This differentiation prompts cultural consequences by producing subcultures that are based on occupational, national, and uniquely historical experiences (Schein, 2017, p. 229). These subcultures need to be understood or else the culture of the organization can change in a negative way, losing its original cultural identity. If you are trying to lead a change initiative in online higher education, say trying to expand the online department and course offerings, these findings below will help you. Even if you aren't in higher education, you will see the similarities between what I'm about to say and with any organization. Schein's work was originally for corporate learning so these next few pages applies to any sector.

Three Subcultures: Operators, Engineers, and Executives

In my experience, online higher education can be defined into three distinctive subcultures. These subcultures are the service-based and student-facing departments (admission's office, registrar's office, academic advising, and faculty), the engineering and design departments (instructional design, course maintenance, and IT support), and senior leadership departments (deans, provosts, and presidents). Interestingly enough, Schein has classified three main subcultures that can be found within any organization and they align to these groups in online higher education. According to Schein (2017), "In every organization in the public or private sector, three generic subcultures must be identified and managed to minimize misalignment or destructive conflict" (p. 221). These generic subcultures are operators, designers, and executives. I would argue that these subcultures align with the roles in online higher education as service-based and student facing departments are operators, the engineering departments are designers, and senior leadership departments are executives. Members in each of these departments possess common assumptions about themselves, the department, and the overall organization. Each assumption provides one extra clue into what they are thinking about, allowing you to understand their perspectives. Let's go over each of these subcultures in detail.

Service-Based and Student Facing Departments – The Operators

The operators are the student-facing departments. They are the ones who sell the organization's products and services, and in this case, it means they are selling the institution's support efforts, values, programs, and courses. Common assumptions among the operator subcultures are:

- The action of any organization is ultimately the action of the people. We are the critical resource; we run the place.

- The success of the enterprise depends on our knowledge, skill, and learning ability, and commitment.

- We know that we will have to deal with unpredictable contingencies.

- We have the capacity to learn, innovate, and deal with surprises.

- We depend on management to give us the proper resources, training, and support to get our jobs done (Schein, 2017, p. 222).

In online higher education, the admission's office, the registrar's office, online instructors, and academic advisors fall into the assumptions above. These departments are based upon human interactions and require a high level of communication, trust, and teamwork to get their jobs done. These departments are the main communication and support system for online students and become essentially the life line for students. It's not surprising for online students to develop strong relationships with these groups and see them as the "face of the institution."

After personally speaking with thousands of online students while working as an academic advisor, it was common to hear this. These students needed to put a face to the name, but with the entire institution. This created a type of bond and identity between the students and these departments. It makes sense, given that the student communicates and interacts with these departments the most. The operator subculture is aware that, no matter how clear the rules are, they are to use their own subjectivity with handling student problems and unpredictable situations. They trust in their own innovative skills to get the job done and to put the students' needs first.

Schein also points out another notable trait in that most employees rarely work to their full capacity except under crisis conditions (2017, p. 222). From my experience, crisis conditions in online higher education mean when a term or semester is starting or concluding, ramping up the work to ensure that students are prepared. Undoubtedly, the pandemic created many of these crisis conditions with trying to maintain adequate support for all students during this time. In my opinion, the emotional and mental exhaustion after these points in time are why working to full capacity year-round would be impossible. With every term/semester start, it felt like a race towards the finish line and it would be unrealistic to sprint the entire time. Higher education is a marathon, not a sprint.

The Engineering and Design Departments – The Engineers

In each organization, there exists one group who represents design elements of the technology underlying the work of the organization, and this group has the knowledge of how the technology is to be utilized (Schein, 2017, p. 224). This subculture can be classified as the engineers. This subculture in particular strongly emphasizes their occupational community and their education. Basic assumptions of engineers include:

- The ideal world is one of elegant machines and processes working in perfect precision and harmony without human intervention.

- People are the problem – they make mistakes and therefore should be designed out of the system wherever possible.

- Solutions must be based on science and available technology.

- Real work involves solving puzzles and overcoming problems.

- Work must be oriented toward useful products and outcomes (Schein, 2017, p. 224).

Instructional designers, course maintenance teams, and IT support can be categorized by these assumptions. These departments have focused on their education and take pride in their work experience and job requirements. To these departments, problems have abstract solutions and can be implemented in the real-world with products and systems that are free of human error. They create products and services that have a purpose, elegance, permanence, efficiency, safety, and aesthetics (Schein, 2017, p. 224). These products are also designed to require standard responses from humans or to have no human operators at all.

All of the points above relate to the design and maintenance of online courses. Instructional designers create courses based on real-world problems and focus on the outcomes of the course. When a course is designed, constructive feedback can be frustrating because the learning experience is different compared to what the instructional designer envisioned. The assumptions also tie into how a course is designed with instructional design models and incorporated learning sciences, best instructional design practices, and different learning models such as competency based, scenario based, self-paced, blended, hybrid, etc.

IT support also falls into the above categories. Most of the errors they run into stem from human error, not the flaws of the institution's website or LMS. IT systems, chat services, and ticketing systems are all utilized to overcome IT problems from online students and must be solved using technology.

Senior Leadership – The Executives

The third subculture that stands above the others is the executives. This subculture is reserved for the CEO and their executives. In the case of online higher education, this means the institution's president and their inner circle. This subculture cares about the necessities for the institution's survival from a financial standpoint and keeping the stakeholders happy.

Ultimately, in higher education, this means graduation rates, enrollment rates, program outcomes, branding, reputation, and other financial perspectives. Basic assumptions of the executives are:

Financial Focus

- Without financial survival and growth, there are no returns to shareholders or to society.

- Financial survival is equivalent to perpetual war with competitors

Self-image Focus: The Embattled Lone Hero

- The economic environment is perpetually competitive and potentially hostile; "in a war, you cannot trust anyone."

- CEO must be the "lone hero," isolated and alone, yet appearing to be in control

- You cannot get reliable data from below because subordinates will tell you what they think you want to hear

- Organization and management are intrinsically hierarchical

- People are a necessary evil

- The well-oiled machine organization does not need whole people, only the activities they are contracted for (Schein, 2017, p. 226).

As you can see from the assumptions above, this subculture comprises of employees who have risen through the rankings to get to where they are today. This includes deans, provosts, and presidents. What was interesting when reading Schein's work on executives is that one position leans closer towards one assumption (Financial Focus or Self-image Focus) than another. Unlike other subcultural assumptions that represent a group holistically, the positions from senior leadership in this subculture are more selective of each assumption.

For instance, provosts tend more towards the "lone hero" assumption with feeling isolated and alone. According to Mark Blegan (2019), provost at Carroll University, "As a provost, you have no peers and report to one person who sits above you on the administrative hierarchy — so finding and solidifying a network of fellow theme-parkers on the provost ride can be a lonely process." This feeling of loneliness can also be seen in comparable school administrator roles for the K-12 environment. According to Dr. Nate Green (2016), an Administrator at the New Hampshire Department of Education, "School administrators are one particular group of professionals who may experience higher than average rates of loneliness as a result of professional isolation" (p. 67).

This feeling of isolation though does not necessarily apply to deans. According to Blegan (2019), "At my previous institution — first as a faculty member and then dean - I could rely on friendships and relationships nurtured over time to help me solve problems, plan strategy, or simply listen when I needed an ear (p. n.a.)." Deans do not seem to have the same troubles as provosts, but they face other obstacles within their roles which apply to finances and the idea that people are a necessary evil. From the financial perspective, it's a dean's responsibility to see the success and well-being of programs that fall into their jurisdiction. If a program produces negative feedback, low success rates, low enrollment rates, and undesirable outcomes, this will all impact the financial survival of the institution and ultimately their job. I'll also include the idea that people are a necessary evil from hearing story after story over the years from deans mentioning grand ideas on how they could improve their existing programs or build new ones, only to be halted by another person or group within the organization.

According to Schein's work, this makes perfect sense. As Schein (2017) stated how executives see people as "impersonal resources that generate problems rather than solutions. People and relationships are viewed as means to the end of efficiency and productivity, not as ends in themselves" (p. 228). I know that these words sound rather harsh, but in my experience, this is the reality when trying to accomplish a task and constantly facing blockers. Presidents tend to fall in between a variety of the executive assumptions. The financial responsibilities certainly weigh on the minds of university presidents, but I think the most compelling assumption would be how it's difficult to receive reliable data because subordinates will try to say what the president wants to hear. The successful presidents I have met have chosen members in their inner circle who will be blunt and straightforward, especially with differing perspectives.

As online higher education grows, more subcultures will develop. Some of the roles mentioned above didn't even exist 10 years ago or have drastically transformed from their previous responsibilities. You can't expect their subcultures to remain the same. It's a leader's job to be able to understand how to navigate and leverage these subcultures. As Schein mentioned, "the leader's task is to find ways of coordinating, aligning, and integrating the different subcultures" (p. 229). If this task is ignored, problems and conflict will rise from the misunderstandings and confusion among these groups. To prevent cultural implosion, leaders in online higher education need to recognize the importance of bringing subcultures together. Building an effective organization is ultimately a matter of meshing the different subcultures by encouraging the evolution of common goals, common language, and common procedures for solving problems' (Schein, 2017, p. 230).

References:

Blegan, M. (2019). What a rookie provost learned in his first semester. https://chroniclevitae.com/news/2215-what-a-rookie-provost-learned-in-his-first-semester

Green, N. (2016). Loneliness and perceived social support in the workplace of the school principal. https://academicarchive.snhu.edu/bitstream/handle/10474/3125/sed2016greene.pdf?sequence=1

Schein, E.H. (2017). *Organizational culture and leadership*. John Wiley and Sons, Inc.

Learning Activities

Practice:

- Identify a member or members of one of the subcultures mentioned above. Ask about their experiences within their environment. Are the assumptions from the subculture aligned with their experiences?

Reflection:

- Think about your own subculture at your organization. What assumptions fairly represent your group?

Chapter 12

WHAT ARE STUDENTS ACTUALLY DOING IN THE COURSE?

There are a few topics that have become embedded into our DNA. You immediately associate topics with a certain term. For instance, when I say the Fourth of July, you most likely think about the American flag, fireworks, and cookouts. You've experienced this event several times in your life, so it makes sense to associate these topics with the holiday. This type of association is actually a cause of concern for online learning.

A typical kick off call on a new project involves talking to faculty members or SMEs about what types of activities and assessments are included in an online course. Nine times out of ten, in my opinion, this involves me dispelling the myths of online learning as just multiple-choice questions and quizzes. While there is nothing wrong with these options, a part of my soul dies every time I hear this. Online learning is over 20 years old at this point in time and the preconceived notion of how students learn is still by multiple choice questions and quizzes.

My problem with these activities isn't the activities themselves, but how they are used. Assessing knowledge by quick checks and quizzes isn't sufficient for building long-term memory. The purpose of multiple-choice questions and quizzes is to strengthen retrieval practice and short-term memory. This is obviously a wonderful technique for learning and should be incorporated in every course; however, they shouldn't be the only assessments. My problem with these is the lack of having students develop their human skills. These activities will not strengthen critical thinking, problem solving, or decision-making abilities. These will assist with remembering terms and concepts, but not applying them into the real world. Think about any decision you have ever made. Did option A, B, C, D, or E magically fall from the sky and you were able to select one of them? I'm guessing probably not. The only time I can think of this happening was in *the Simpsons Movie* (2007). President Schwarzenegger was tasked to deal with a pollution issue at Lake Springfield and he was given 5 choices from his advisor. In the real world, students won't have 5 choices laid out in front of them on solving problems. They have to first think of the potential solutions and then critically think on what the best outcome could be with each solution.

Once again, I'm not telling you to remove these options from your courses or never use them again. I actually did remove them for one of my pilot programs and students freaked out. They have become so engrained into the tradition of online courses that they thought something was wrong. I had students connecting with me in a panic thinking that the course somehow malfunctioned since there weren't multiple-choice questions. I learned my lesson about removing them altogether and found better ways to incorporate them into the lesson plans.

So, what exactly are students doing in the course in order to build critical thinking, decision making, and problem-solving skills? I'm so glad you asked! My team and I at MIT had this same question. We were tasked with creating a technical leadership program and the purpose of the program was to focus on these types of skills. The content in the program had to be transferrable from the classroom to the workplace. In order to ensure that all of the courses in the program were designed cohesively, we created a pedagogical model that would deliver the best learning experience. The inspiration came from MIT's motto, *mens et manus*, meaning mind and hand (2021). This motto had stood the test of time by believing in promoting education for practical application. This meant that the technical leader program had to comprise of active learning strategies and hands-on activities that applied to the real-world. Research from evidenced-based instructional design practices, learning sciences, and neuroscience, as well as decades of digital learning research at MIT led to the creation of our learning model called, MIT xPRO Pedagogical Model.

This pedagogical model emphasized doing over consuming.

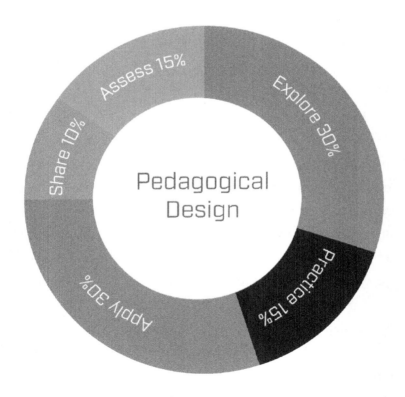

Figure 12.1: Pedagogical Model

This design was segmented into 5 areas: exploring, practicing, applying, sharing, and assessing. Each learning element of what students performed in the online program is explained below:

- Explore: Engaging videos, research-based papers and articles, podcasts, and webinars
- Practice: Ungraded multiple-choice questions, drag and drop, scenario problems, and simulation activities
- Apply: Case studies, essays, self-reflections, and journals
- Share: Peer-to-peer discussions, surveys, polls
- Assess: Pre- and post-assessments, peer assessment tools, summative assessment instruments

This model became the framework for how to design the student learning experience. By taking different learning techniques and connecting them with the course content, students learned about tangible skills for the work force. Each of these learning elements provided opportunities to incorporate learning techniques such as scenario-based learning, project-based learning, gamification, role playing, group-based, and more. The goal was to have students participate at least 70% of the time in creating an active learning experience. For your courses, a general rule would be to think about how many hours a week students are spending on the material and then to plan the experience around that. For instance, let's say the goal is to have students complete a week's worth of content within 5 hours. Students, on average, should spend 1 hour watching videos and reading articles. The remaining 4 hours should have students actively participating in the course. This timeframe will certainly fluctuate depending on the product you are designing, but it's a start for how to think about the overall learning experience and what students are actually doing.

References:

Brooks, J. L., Groening, M., Jean, A., Scully, M., Sakai, R., Maxtone-Graham, I., Meyer, G., ... Copyright Collection (Library of Congress). (2007). *The Simpsons movie*. Beverly Hills, Calif: 20th Century Fox Home Entertainment.

Hobson, L., Carramolino ,B., Bagiati, A., Haldi, T., & Roy, A. (2020) TEACHING AND LEARNING TECHNICAL AND MANAGERIAL LEADERSHIP SKILLS THROUGH SCENARIO-BASED LEARNING. Retrieved from: https://www.sefi.be/wp-content/uploads/2020/11/Proceedings-DEF-nov-2020-kleiner.pdf

MIT Libraries (2021). Retrieved from: https://libraries.mit.edu/mithistory/institute/seal-of-the-massachusetts-institute-of-technology/

Learning Activities

Practice:

- Think of one of the courses you designed or one of the courses you have participated in. Using the learning model, map out what activities aligned to which areas. How many hours a week did you spend on each?

Reflection:

- Think back to your favorite course. What activities did you do that made you feel like you were part of the learning process?

Chapter 13

HOW DO I WORK WITH SMES?

The most effective online courses are designed by instructional designers and Subject Matter Experts (SMEs) who are on the same page. When these two parties both feel that they have an equal voice in the conversation and they establish a partnership, the best possible learning experience is achieved. Notice how I particularly said the word "equal" because I've seen power struggles on both sides with the SME attempting to block every attempt with change or the opposite with having the ID team limit the creativity of the SME all together. It is crucial from the very beginning to be on the same page and not let chaos ensue; proper boundaries and guidelines must be followed for the project to run smoothly. If I had to pick only one thing to teach you from my ID experiences, it would be this chapter. The art of negotiating, influencing, and persuading with SMEs will help you more than anything else. That human skill set will make a project successful. A true instructional designer is a relationship manager.

Learning More About SMEs

First things first, let's talk about SMEs. Who are they? These are experts in their respective fields. They understand the subject matter like the back of their hands and their experiences could come from academia, on the job experiences, or a mix of both. For those of you working in higher education, your SMEs are most likely faculty members or hired adjunct instructors. For those of you in corporate, non-profit, a government agency, etc. your SMEs could be experts in the industry or trainers of experts in the industry. I've found the learning experience to be the best when you can combine both academic and industry experience to have several perspectives for students to learn from. It makes the course content relatable to anyone taking the course and makes the content more robust.

One of my mistakes early on in my career was not conducting research before meeting my SMEs. It was normal for me to be assigned to work with a SME and then have a kick off call to do introductions and talk more about how we were going to work on the project together. I noticed after a few of these kick off calls that they always had a bit of awkwardness to them. You don't know these SMEs and they don't know you. It's almost like being set up on a blind date. Imagine being in their shoes where they have been told to work with a person they don't know, they don't have a clue what instructional design means, they don't fully grasp the impact of online learning, they've never seen a well-designed online course, and potentially have even more hesitations about the project. This happened to me multiple times; I'd go in thinking about how I was about to have a pleasant conversation with someone and instead, ended up playing 21 questions with them to try and build my credibility on the spot. Eventually, I grew tired of this mental battle and decided to start conducting research on SMEs beforehand, and wow, this literally changed the game for me!

Here is what I started to do and still do to this day. After you've been assigned to work with a SME, look up their name on LinkedIn. Look at their education, their past posts, and see if they have a professional website listed. You can also search on Google to find blogs and articles or YouTube to find lectures. Whatever content is out there, try to learn what they are passionate about. This research will give you some more insight on who the SME is, what's important to them, and most importantly, it will let you understand their terminology. For instance, if I have been assigned to work on a new course, I want to familiarize myself with the field specific terms the SME is going to use. This will let you make an instant connection with the SME and shows that you have put in the extra effort to learn more about their field. I've found that this process reduces the perception that you are a novice and builds credibility quickly.

Years ago, I was assigned to work with a SME on a new business strategies course. As you can imagine, this is quite a broad topic and I had no prior documentation on which direction the course was going to go in. To help narrow my search, I tried to learn more about my SME and looked him up on LinkedIn, where he listed his own professional website that had his bio and more around his philosophy on business and education. On his site, he mentioned a few recent published articles all around business strategies and that's when I dove in. Yes, these were massive white papers, but I was determined to try to learn as much as I could about these topics. By the time I had my kick off call with him, I felt prepared. As we started to chat, I could tell that he had a stressful day and the last thing he wanted to do was to teach me about the topics he wanted to cover. This is when I eagerly jumped in and said, "By the way, I read your last few papers." He looked at me in astonishment and said, "…you did?" I then gave a brief summary of one of them and talked about how I could see it translate into an online practice activity. He was floored. This one act of researching allowed us to create a working relationship in minutes and we were on the same page with everything about the design process after this.

The next time you are assigned to work with a SME try this:

- Research SME's Name
  - LinkedIn
  - Personal Website
    - Interviews
    - Journals
    - Blogs
    - Articles
    - YouTube Videos
    - Podcasts
      - Learn Terminology, Perspectives, Mindset, Passions

If you are able to do this, you'll be one step ahead of the game.

Explaining Your Role

When you have your first call with a SME, it's of the utmost importance that you explain your role on the project. Any seasoned instructional designer will tell you that they have worked with SMEs before who didn't understand the purpose of the instructional design role. SMEs will typically go right into a teaching mindset (as they most likely have taught this course before) and it's entirely possible that they have a misconception of what an ID is there to help with. You can simply ask if they know what an instructional designer does and if they answer with yes, have them explain their perceptions of the job. Whatever their answer is, I like to frame my job description to them of why I'm on these projects. Here is what I say every single time, "I understand how people learn. Using this knowledge, I work with a SME, like yourself, to create a meaningful learning experience. This leads me to designing and developing curricula, resources, and materials that link to course outcomes, competences, and skills." This statement explains that you are here to contribute in several ways to make the online learning experience the best it can possibly be. This statement also helps in reducing misconceptions of the role.

Explaining your role also helps SMEs to understand where their work starts and stops. Depending upon their personality and dedicated time to the project, they might do too much or too little. I've had a SME before send me hundreds upon hundreds of slide decks thinking that was all I needed to make a great course. I've also experienced the opposite with another SME essentially doing my job and theirs, and still worrying that they weren't working hard enough. Explaining your role will establish these required boundaries and expectations.

■ Understanding Their Preferences

As instructional designers, we are the ones who take ownership of a project. We set the pace and tone from the kick off calls to talk about project scopes to weekly check-ins. When you are first beginning to work with a SME, it's important to listen to their preferences before you get into a rhythm. Most IDs are methodical, organized, and strategic. Not every person works like this and some SMEs are only productive with drop dead deadlines. It's your job to understand their working preferences and to try to adapt them into your normal workflow.

Here's an example of a mistake I made early on. I was assigned to work on developing a new course with the dean serving as my SME and eventually, she would teach it too. This was the first time I had worked with someone who would be filling in as both the SME and professor and to add more pressure, she was after all, the dean of the department. When we met, I explained about my process of how I design online courses and went immediately into setting up recurring check ins. As I popped up my calendar, I could tell that she looked worried. I stopped myself and realized that I only told her about how I prefer to work. I talked about my system. I had heard that this person was tough to work with so I immediately went into a mindset of taking ownership of the flow of the project. I then took a step back and asked her to tell me how she usually works on her projects. This led me to understanding her current schedule, when she had time to do the work, and just how she works in general. I was accustomed to working on a project in small increments each day, where she preferred to dedicate one day where she could solely focus on the course. I pivoted and adopted the way she preferred to work while blending some of my methods into the workflow. We found the flow that worked well with both of our preferences.

For your introduction calls, I would ask about their schedule, how they prefer to work, and what tools (Email, Google Sheets, Zoom, etc.) they currently use. All of these topics will let you know how to modify your approach.

Providing Examples

This step is usually overlooked by instructional designers and I honestly can't figure out why. SMEs and faculty members aren't any different from other people when it comes to being persuading or influenced by a product. When a typical consumer is thinking about making an investment into a project, they want to see the end results first. Think of how if a consumer were to hire a contractor to remodel their kitchen. Chances are, the first step the consumer does is search the contractor's website for their portfolio to see examples of beautifully designed kitchens. The course design process is the same way. Show your SME an example of a finished course and walk them through the design process.

This will provide a visual and they can now imagine what their own course will look like in the future.

Providing demos of courses is significant in two ways. First, this establishes your credibility. For many projects, instructional designers and SMEs will have never met before. They aren't familiar with your work and vice versa. SMEs get a little bit more benefit of the doubt that they know what they are doing with their years of experience and teaching. Instructional designers have to prove their worth. Showcasing a finished product will absolutely do it. This also has a great side effect of making the SME excited to design the course. It's one thing just to talk about what the finished course will look like. It's another when you can make the SME imagine themselves with their name contributing to a fantastic course.

While you are presenting these finished courses, you are inevitably dispelling myths about what online courses are and are not. SMEs and faculty members will typically have a belief of what online courses should entail, either from past experience or from conversations. From my personal experience, many of them still believe that online courses only consist of readings, videos, discussion posts, and essays. Obviously, there are far more ways instructional designers can make online courses engaging. During the demo is a great time to encourage the SME or faculty member to ask questions and talk about the design process. This provides a sense of understanding for what they will be contributing to the course and how everything will come together in the end.

Creating Instructions

There is an incredibly high chance that your SME will be working with you on a part-time basis. They'll care about the project, but this isn't their full-time job. In order to use their time wisely, you'll want to reduce any potential barriers when it comes to working together. An easy step in the right direction is to create simple instructions for them to follow.

For many SMEs, this is their first time designing a course and you need to lead them towards the goal. For instance, many instructional designers start the course design process by following a model like Backward Design by Wiggins and McTighe. This model prioritizes the course outcomes and then works backwards to make the assessments, learning activities, and course content. In order to start this process, you need to provide clear instructions to the SME on how to make a proper course outcome. I always start with the basic question, "What should students learn and be able to do at the end of the course?" It's a simple question that gets the conversation started and then you can work together to make the outcomes clear.

These simple instructions should be incorporated when you are using templates or looking for feedback. I primarily use Google Docs and Google Sheets when working with

SMEs. Within these docs and sheets, I already have guiding questions in place for the SMEs to fill out. Here are a few examples:

- Which course-level outcomes align to this section?
- What skills are the students using?
- Why are they using these skills?
- How would they successfully demonstrate these skills?

When I comment on their work to leave feedback, I try to be as clear as possible for what I'm looking for.

Setting Deadlines and Recurring Meetings

As mentioned before, SMEs are busy people. You need to be on their radar and stay on their radar until the course is complete. To do this, you need to create a project timeline and a timeline on deliverables. The project timeline will be your guiding document and will leave no room for doubt over what is due and when. I send this to my SMEs as soon as possible for them to plan ahead. Your deadlines could be weekly or bi-weekly. It all depends on the size and scope of the project. You should have separate deadlines for each part of the course (creating assessments, video recording, reviewing materials, etc.). The video recording process will be longer compared to working on a short assignment, so factor these into the deadlines.

This may seem excessive, but I would recommend scheduling a weekly 30-minute Zoom call. These recurring meetings will keep both you and the SME on track. I've had some SMEs fill out the course outline, Backward Design template or other templates while I was on the call with them since they didn't feel comfortable filling out the templates alone. I've had other SMEs who completed everything and our calls were simply to review and critique the work. Figure out how the SME prefers to work and adapt to their style to best support them. One last thing: if the SME pushes back by saying the recurring meetings aren't necessary, explain the benefits of them and the likely consequences of not having them.

Providing Feedback

One common mistake when working with SMEs is the belief that they don't want feedback. That is simply not true. SMEs need the appropriate feedback on their work. Is it possible that they are reluctant to hear it? Sure. Is the feedback necessary to design the best learning experience? Yes. I was working with one SME and provided coaching while he was filming his videos. While he recorded his videos with an iPhone, I was muted on Zoom and would provide my feedback after each take. This SME was an absolute professional and did phenomenally with each take, so I wasn't providing as much constructive feedback as normal. After his third video, he asked for my honest opinion and to not just tell him he was doing a great job. It caught me by surprise, but then I realized he was looking for specific feedback on *why* he was doing a great job so he could highlight those parts more in the other videos. I then went into detail about how he provided fantastic introductions and conclusions, explained each step thoroughly, provided examples, and highlighted pit falls. Sure enough, he used this feedback in the rest of the videos. Even the best SMEs are looking to make sure that they are on track.

You'll also work with SMEs who are doing well in the design process, but they need a bit of extra coaching to make the work finalized. For these SMEs, try asking thought-provoking questions to make them think about the material in a different way. One strategy is to say, "Help me understand this part more. What do you mean by XYZ concept?" Most instructional designers will ask SMEs to teach them the content, but if the content still isn't finalized after that, they face a road block. One strategy I love to use to get around this is to make the SME think of when they taught the content to a struggling student. Don't just think about the average student who will get it right on the first try. How would you teach this to a student who still didn't understand the first approach? This will make the SME think of other ways to teach the same content and will usually lead to new ideas for both you and the SME.

Knowing When to Pushback

Now that we've covered working with great SMEs, let's talk about the elephant in the room: working with unresponsive SMEs. The overwhelming majority of SMEs are lovely to work with, but any instructional designer can tell you they have worked with an incredibly challenging SME before. Some of the reasons could be:

- Forced on the project by their supervisor

- Doesn't accept criticism

- Doesn't believe in the project

- Didn't have the time to begin with, but accepted the position

- Lost interest in the idea

Whatever the reason, the fact of the matter is that the SME is assigned to the project and you need to figure out how to work with them. There have been a few times in my career where I needed to pull the SME aside and have a private conversation on what was wrong. While they were unpleasant to have, the conversations gave clear direction on what we needed to do and if we couldn't meet in the middle, we would be going our separate ways. One time, I had a SME refuse to accept my criticism for the course. He felt that his topics were vital to the students' success, but I kept on repeating that these topics were unnecessary. Long story short, the student feedback highlighted my points and the whole course had to be redesigned working with new SMEs. I did everything within my power (and so did my director) to try and fix the problem, but he flat out refused. While this led to spending more time, energy, and resources to redesign the course, everyone else on the project was glad to have the heads up that things weren't going well. Even the SME's supervisor was shocked at what happened and said that it was out of character for him. There are always factors that we won't be aware of, so try to keep an open mind and think about their perspective.

Learning Activities

Practice:

- Instructional designers often find themselves in a position where they have to explain their roles and how they help with the course design process. Another significant piece is also debunking myths on what instructional designers are not. In your own words, describe your interpretation of what an instructional designer does and how you can help a SME with the design process. Be sure to include details on how you will contribute to the project.

Reflection:

- While it's crucial to know how your SME likes to work, it's also important to know your own style. How do you prefer to work on projects? Describe your work preferences for timing, communication styles, meetings, tools, and anything else that comes to mind.

Chapter 14

HOW DO I KNOW IF MY COURSES ARE DESIGNED WELL?

With the final push of the publish button, your online course is live! A sense of accomplishment and relief take over and you can take a deep breath for the first time in weeks. Any instructional designer will say how the days, hours, and minutes leading up to launching a course are stressful. Just because the course is live doesn't mean that the job is done. What if certain materials don't resonate with students? What if the directions aren't as easy to follow as you thought? This is where the course improvement process begins. Collecting, analyzing, and applying student feedback can and will enhance the learning experience. So, how do you navigate this process and where do you start? I'll explain each step in this improvement process for what I have done for my online courses and programs. Before we begin, though, you need to have the right mindset to do this.

Online education is an ever-evolving process. Just because a technique worked years ago doesn't mean that it will always be effective. You need to understand that students know best. They are the ones who have experienced your course and their words can give you the necessary guidance to make improvements. Be open minded with the idea of changing the content to better serve your audience. It's easy to be defensive of your work, and that's why I'm asking you to let down your guard a little. If you truly believe that you are right, you'll have to do more research to understand why the content isn't connecting with your students. It could possibly be a small revision that will make the stars align. Either way, keep an open mind as your students are not making these remarks to be hurtful, but are providing suggestions to make the course even better.

Creating a Pilot Program

Depending upon where you are in your course's timeline, a pilot may or may not be feasible. If you have enough time, I would always recommend conducting a pilot program. Why? Pilot programs provide critical information ahead of time before the launch of the course and will provide clarity on areas of opportunity. Most instructional designers will review their own courses before the launch date and will ask their colleagues to do the same. This is a great practice for catching quick fixes; however, these colleagues are not your intended audience. Just because they understand your instructions doesn't mean that your students will.

To give you an example, my team conducted a pilot program on a series of <u>online technical leadership courses</u>. The IDs on the team went through the pilot program and identified areas for improvement. When the students went through the program, though, they identified different areas and actually loved some of the content that the other designers wanted to revise. This happened because the students had different perspectives compared to the IDs. Paying closer attention towards their wants allowed us to better speak their language and focus on what truly mattered. If you are able to conduct a pilot, you'll need enough time to implement the changes, so expect anywhere for a 3-6-month turnaround, as these revisions will be on top of your other typical responsibilities.

Using a Mixed Methods Approach

There are multiple ways to approach collecting and analyzing data. It all comes down to what the project calls for in regards to time, energy, and resources. If your project only needs some fine tuning, then a small sample size for a qualitative or quantitative approach could get the job done. My personal favorite is to do an explanatory sequential mixed methods approach. That's essentially a design in which the researcher begins by conducting a quantitative phase first and follows up on specific results with a qualitative phase. The qualitative phase is implemented for the purposes of explaining the initial results in more depth; this focus on explaining results is reflected in the design name (Creswell & Plano Clark, 2011, p. 82). You can see the framework below:

Figure 14.1: Explanatory Sequential Mixed Methods Approach

Basically, start with a survey (quan approach) and then use the survey findings to influence how you'll structure the interview questions (qual approach). The answers to these interview questions will provide an overall explanation you can use for revising the course's content. This design certainly has its challenges and advantages. As you can probably guess, the challenge here is that this process takes time. To me, it's worth it because the advantage of this style over others is the level of high-quality feedback you can use for improving your course. A mixed methods approach will also provide you more opportunities to ask questions and dig deeper than just surface-level answers. For example, let's say you anticipated your students answering the survey questions in one manner and instead, they answered the complete opposite way. You will obviously want to know more about these responses instead of making an educated guess as to what happened. This mixed approach creates an opportunity for you to dig deeper and find out more information behind the unexpected survey findings.

Designing the Survey (Quan)

For designing the survey structure, keep it simple by using 1-5 Likert scales and multiple-choice questions. You can use different scales for assessment, such as highly engaging to not engaging, highly valuable to not valuable, strongly agree to strongly disagree, etc. I'd also recommend a "tell us anything" section in the survey to let the students do a brain dump of anything they thought about the course so far. This is normally a big no-no in best research practices, but since this is an exploratory practice, the more information you can get about their experiences, the better. I know that for many IDs and teachers, who have been working around the clock due to COVID-19, the survey is also a great place to ask if the students encountered any bugs, errors, or anything platform-related. It's really easy to miss a typo or a similar mistake if you are producing course after course and running on only coffee and will power. Lastly, since you will be conducting interviews afterwards, make sure there is a question about conducting a follow up with the students! If you don't have this section, it means you won't know who to contact.

For creating the survey content, try to only ask important questions. I know this sounds like an obvious statement, but we have all taken a survey before that took what felt like an eternity to answer. Make these questions quick and succinct. You can ask questions about their behavioral patterns, content being relatable, learning behaviors, etc. One question that you should always ask as an ID or teacher is how long it took the students to complete the module. In my experience, this is the question that can produce answers you weren't expecting. When my colleague and I were developing one of the courses in the leadership program, we were blown away by how long it was taking some learners while others were taking the expected amount of time. This became an excellent question to ask more about in the qualitative portion to hear their stories and uncover what they were experiencing.

Collecting the Data in the LMS

What's the best way to start the data collection process? First, you need a type of survey tool. My favorite is Qualtrics because of its back-end customization and easy to read reports, but Google forms will also get the job done. Once your survey is complete, embed the link at the end of each module/week in your LMS.

You will want to include a survey for each module for "real time" feedback. Trying to ask students to provide feedback on all of the course's content at the end of the term/semester will only give you an overview, but won't provide specifics for each week. It's simply too much information to store, retrieve, and critique. You want the feedback while it's still fresh in their minds. I'd also recommend to make the survey required so that way you have enough responses to make an educated decision based on the feedback. If you have a classroom full of 25 students and only 2 provide feedback, it's not as helpful compared to a higher number.

Analyzing the Survey Results

Once your survey responses are in, download the results via PDF formatting. It's the easiest and cleanest way to read the data and to share it with appropriate stakeholders. Carefully observe the answers to each question and look for overarching patterns. Take note of the majority of answers for each question and see if there are any results that are surprising. You are looking for discrepancies among the data. Did one week receive heavy favoritism over another? Did students respond better to projects instead of other assignments? Was there more class participation at one interval of time compared to another? Look for these differences and find the ones that you can't explain. For instance, I mentioned earlier how learners were devoting drastically different amounts of time in the module. This is a great example of something we couldn't explain and we marked it down as a follow up question we wanted to learn more about. If you really want to be nerdy and precise with the quantitative data, you can find the mean, median, mode, and standard deviation. Depending upon your goal, it could be helpful, but this is certainly not needed in every instance.

At this point in time, reach out to the students who said they would be willing to participate in a follow up interview. You should be sending these invites while the survey is still fresh in their minds and you can reserve time on the calendar now to save that appointment. Coordinating schedules between several people easily takes the most amount of time from this entire process, so plan ahead!

Developing Interview Questions

From here, you can start to develop your interview questions. Your interview questions should all be open-ended and specific. For instance, here is a poor example of an interview question: *"Did you enjoy the content from Week 1?"* Here is an example of a thought-provoking question:

"Week 1 was conceived as a basic overview of the course and was the lowest rated week on the feedback surveys. How could the content have been presented differently? What content or activities do you feel could have improved the experience?" Did you notice the differences between the questions? In the first question, all you will receive is a yes or no type of answer. In the second question, you are asking students to recall the week, their feelings, and how the learning experience can be enhanced.

Also, get as granular as you would like if it's appropriate for your audience. I've found that when I conduct interviews and share the survey results with students in real-time, they find it enjoyable and want to participate more in the research. For instance, in my dissertation, I would cite percentages to back up my claims. One of my questions for students asked, "About 34% of Millennial Generation students answered that their advisor does not demonstrate concern for their social development. Why do you think they feel that way?" (Hobson, 2019). This type of question helped them remember the survey and how they answered. You could say the same with course questions like, "The majority of students said that Week 4 was their favorite week and that it was the most relevant to their job. Why was Week 4 more relevant compared to the other weeks and how would you like to see the other weeks become more relevant to your job?" Have about 8-10 questions ready to go for the interviews.

Hosting the Interview Sessions (Qual)

Now the fun begins! You will learn so much in a short amount of time. From my experience, the course improvement process can be more effective by hosting small focus groups. I've found that students in small groups like 3-4 people can have a great conversation with each question bringing about several unique perspectives. Most of the time, when one student answers, another student wants to comment and make a point or counterpoint. Having more than this number makes the interview process difficult to navigate, however. Not only do you need to be a facilitator for several people, you need to prepare for unexpected issues like Wi-Fi problems, microphone glitches, or some other technology issue, assuming you will be conducting your meeting through one of the video sharing platforms. It's not impossible to manage a larger group, but I'd advise you to host several small groups.

Have a script prepared for everything you are going to be talking about. Here's my structure:

- Opening Statement (Thanking them for their time, purpose of the interview, etc.)
- Introduction
- Interview Questions
- Closing Remarks

This structure creates a smooth transition from each part of the focus group. Consider recording this if it's allowed and everyone attending the group is comfortable with it. This will allow you to go back and listen for smaller detailers you may have missed. I'd also strongly advise that you have another colleague take notes for you while you are conducting the interviews. This will allow you to pay closer attention to your students' words and may lead to more questions. Trying to do the hosting and note taking duties at the same time usually leads to overlooking significant details.

Interpreting the Results

You now have all of the data you are looking for! Congrats! Review all of the answers from the focus groups and categorize the answers into their appropriate themes. Earlier, I mentioned themes such as behavioral patterns, content being relatable, and learning behaviors, just to give you an example. This categorization process will give you a clearer perspective of how all of the data links together from the course content to the survey to the interview findings. You can then draw conclusions based on all of these elements. Sometimes, you'll find that many comments align from each group and it's a crystal clear answer of what students would like to see improved. Other times, it takes more effort and your experiences can guide you. I'll give you an example of an easy solution and an example that took more time to think about.

For the easy one, after conducting 3 focus groups, we heard from learners that they wanted a way to take notes online as they progressed through their course. We were assuming that they could just use a Word doc or pen and paper to take notes, but students wanted a template to follow. My team and I came up with a "key takeaway" document that let students fill in notes on pre-populated information for each week. It was a no brainer and students loved it.

For one idea that took more time to develop, we heard that students were looking for additional resources besides readings and videos. Given that most additional resources are either articles or videos, we had to get creative with this one. We decided to make a podcast based around the course's content and embedded the podcast player into the course's resource section. We chose this method as our targeted audience were busy adults whose demographics aligned with the typical podcast listener. We found out it was a success when students were raving about it in the discussion boards in the LMS.

Applying the Changes

At this point, you have your ideas outlined for improving the learning experience in your course. With all of your ideas, I would use some tactic when it comes to project management like a <u>Trello board</u>, Google Sheet, or you could be old school like me and use a white board. For each change, create an estimated time frame of how long it will take. For this process, be 100% honest with yourself and your schedule. If one change is going to take 3-6 months, then so be it. Overpromising on these changes can completely ruin the intention of revising the course in the first place. Make the learning experience the priority.

References:

Creswell, J. W., & Plano Clark, V. L. (2011). *Designing and conducting mixed methods research*. Thousand Oaks, California: SAGE Publications, Inc.

Hobson, L. A. (2019) *Understanding online millennial generation students' relationship perceptions with online academic advisors*

Learning Activities

Practice:

- Imagine yourself receiving negative feedback about your course structure, design, or content. What would it take for you to change your mind about the course design? What approach would you take to accept this criticism and not let yourself become biased with the results?

Reflection:

- Think of a time you made an assumption about your students' understanding of a subject and then realized it was inaccurate. How did you adjust your content based on this new information? If you haven't encountered this before, imagine yourself in this type of situation. Describe your strategy for adjusting the design.

Chapter 15

WHAT DOES THE DAY IN THE LIFE OF AN INSTRUCTIONAL DESIGNER LOOK LIKE?

"What does an instructional designer actually do?" A quick Google search will pop up some amazing videos, podcasts, and blogs about a day in the life of an instructional designer from a corporate perspective or a freelance perspective. I didn't see the same types of results though for higher education, and I have an educated guess as to why: it's ridiculously hard to describe the typical day.

You see, I've been meaning to cover this topic for almost a year; however, I couldn't think of the right way of conveying my day-to-day. Since I'm an ID in higher education, my life revolves around the seasons of the year or different quarters. One would assume that my day job would be relatively slow in the summer, but in reality, it's my busiest time. I'm wearing my creative thinking hat to design all of my programs and to put the finishing touches on them before they go live in the fall. This naturally means that my mentality in the fall changes, where I put my design skills on the backburner and instead focus on logistics with uploading the content to the LMS, QA testing the functionalities, making sure the programs are properly staffed/trained, etc.

So, trying to describe the typical day is quite challenging. This post is my best effort though of capturing a snapshot of my life as a Senior Instructional Designer and Program Manager at MIT. I will note that your day-to-day could be completely different in another institution. There are so many factors that need to be accounted for that could change an instructional designer's responsibilities. For instance, a few items that can and will change the role are budget, scope of the projects, size of the immediate team, and other factors. My team is relatively small, so I have to wear many hats. What I'm going to describe might be different for you, but at least this will give you a general sense of an instructional designer's responsibilities within higher education.

Research

Since I'm talking about MIT, research has to be involved. I'm not talking about advanced robots or finding the cures to viruses, though. When I say research, I'm referring to the idea of a new program, the relevancy of the topic to the workforce, and the effectiveness of the designed material from the learner's perspective.

Let's first talk about how research is involved in coming up for the concept of a new program. There are programs out there on every single topic imaginable. How do you decide which ones to pursue? That's where research comes into play. An idea will be brought forward from an internal member of the team or from an instructor, director, or dean. At this point in time, the idea needs to vetted. The program concept could be incredibly interesting, but if the target population for the program aren't using education to solve the problem, no one is going to enroll. To determine the likelihood of enrollment, different points of data are utilized from Google and EMSI/ Burning Glass. Experts in the field and other educators are also contacted to gauge the interest of the program's concept. This has been a fascinating part of the job because I love connecting with others and hearing how they are currently approaching problems that I can then bring back into the program's design. For instance, when I was developing a course on <u>Critical Thinking and Decision Making</u> for engineers, I used my network and connected with different kinds of engineers who the program would be designed for. This allowed me to gain a sense of how engineers viewed the concept of critical thinking and how their employers communicated the importance of critical thinking.

There is a fair amount of research at the end of the design phase of a program too. For my programs, I conduct a pilot program before they go live and in my pilots, I collect survey data at the end of each week, look for discrepancies I can't explain, then host focus groups or individual interviews to dive in deeper into these topics, which then helps me form my overall conclusion of how I'm going to change the design.

To give you an example of this, I can stick with the program of Critical Thinking and Decision Making. I designed this program in early 2020. Other countries were beginning to work remotely and I could sense that it was only a matter of time until this happened in the United States. I had a premonition that this was going to happen globally so I designed a problem where the learners had to envision themselves as a manager who had to use their critical thinking skills in order to determine when it would be safe to let employees go back to work in-person. I interviewed the pilot program's learners afterwards and they were amazed at how relevant this problem was to their role as they experienced remote life at the exact same time as completing the program. Many of these learners served on committees who had to tackle this problem in the real world and this problem absolutely resonated with them. Needless to say, this research process has made me grow leaps and bounds when it comes to creating the course assessments, activities, and exploratory content.

The final comment I have on research is writing research papers and presenting at conferences. This is fairly common in higher education and if you enjoy writing or public speaking, it's a fun part of the job. You can read the white paper I've referenced written by my colleagues and I on scenario-based learning.

Design

The term "design" is in instructional designer after all, so it's safe to say that designing has to be in the typical day. How much you design will certainly change depending upon your organization and even your style. Personally, I like to design everything so when you click through each page and see the readings, activities, and assessments, I had a hand in creating them. The same can be said for creating the learning outcomes and program description. Someone has to think about what the learner's journey is going to be like from reading the "Welcome" page all the way until they submit their final assignment. This process of being able to map out every single item the learner is going to experience is a part of being an instructional designer.

Let me stress this important point: an instructional designer should not be doing this alone. One question that

I answer every week is, "Do I need to be an expert in XYZ subject to design a course on it?" The answer is a resounding no. Leadership courses are my sweet spot, but I've worked on courses about 3D printing, AI, and Cybersecurity. I'm not the expert on any of those topics. This is why it's so important to <u>develop meaningful relationships with subject matter experts (SMEs)</u>. The SMEs, in my case, are usually professors, recent graduates, and industry experts. Working with SMEs is an essential part of the design process to ensure that what you are describing in the program actually makes sense. A humungous part of my role is to be transparent with learners in showing how the content aligns from the learning outcomes, to the assessments, to the activities, and to the readings and videos. I want learners to understand the purpose of why they are doing something in the program and to never experience feeling like the content isn't going to be beneficial in the real world. Working with SMEs can help to illustrate these points.

Speaking of SMEs, one additional part to my role is partnering with the multimedia team and filming the SMEs. In my programs, professors and industry experts are filmed to share their knowledge and to provide both perspectives of academia and industry. Before these filming sessions, I outline the topics with SMEs to ensure that we touch upon each item for the designed week. Some SMEs ask for help with scripting these ideas while others come prepared with PPT decks. During the filming sessions, I'm attentively listening to how they share their knowledge and provide feedback along the way. Sitting in on these sessions has been vital to my job. I've had some SMEs completely forget to talk about certain topics or bring up brand new topics that we didn't discuss. Some SMEs were nervous on camera and needed a bit of extra coaching to get them through the day. Whatever somebody needs as far as for feedback, guidance, and coaching, that's why I'm there.

Communication

As much as I would love to say that design is the core of my role, I could make an argument that communication is the most significant component. My life revolves around Slack, Zoom, and Outlook. Even before working remotely, I still used the tools constantly. When I'm creating a program, I'm in touch with everyone at all times. I'm only one cog in the machine, after all. There are other departments who need to be included in the design process such as marketing, multimedia, engineering, and customer support. I also obviously need to keep in close contact with my SMEs and my team members. If anything unexpected happens during the program's progress, I have to inform the appropriate stakeholders. For instance, if the program's progress is delayed, I would need to tell the marketing folks right away about the issue. If a SME wanted to use a specific simulation, I would need to ensure that it worked with our platform and consult the engineering team, run the numbers by marketing and finance, provide FAQs to customer support, and more. Everyone appreciates being in the loop and I try to do this as much as humanly as possible.

Another significant part of my role is public speaking. This isn't typical for an instructional designer, but it has transformed my position. Public speaking is such a valuable ability and I beg you to start working on this skill. I mentioned before about presenting research at conferences, but that's only a few times per year. Where I use my public speaking skills the most is with running meetings, presenting to different departments, performing a demo for another organization, sharing information with other universities, and other events. One unexpected bonus about public speaking has been my interactions with learners. The other day, one of our programs kicked off and someone had to run the webinar to welcome new learners. I volunteered because I was excited to welcome them into the program and to talk more about what they were going to experience for the next couple of months. I'm confident in saying that the more you grow in the instructional design space, the more you'll need public speaking skills.

Management

Last, but not least is management. Managing projects and relationships is a typical part of my day. As you read earlier in this post, my title does have the term "Program Manager" in there for good measure. Once the programs have been designed, it's my task to ensure they run smoothly. This includes checking the build within the LMS, hiring the staff, fixing bugs, responding to escalated questions, and other similar instances. Essentially, all maintenance and operations of programs are my responsibility.

Managing relationships is going to round out this list. By relationships, I mean creating partnerships with SMEs, vendors, and online program managers (OPMs). Maintaining relationships with SMEs is key to the job. Without a healthy relationship, the project could fall off the rails quickly. If you are new to working with SMEs, my video will help you. In regards to vendors and OPMs, it's extremely common in the ID field to work with other organizations. They can be incredibly beneficial if you lack the people power or the time for projects. Throughout my career, I've found myself being in the position of overseeing projects and providing feedback before signing off on them. It's like being the middle person between two organizations and making sure that everyone is satisfied with the end result. Working alongside vendors and OPMs has been quite the learning process. They don't report to you and you don't report to them, but you are in the projects together. Without a mutual level of respect and a healthy balance of giving and receiving feedback, your projects will fall apart. From connecting with many vendors and OPMs over the years, my advice is to do your research when it comes to working together. Figure out their strengths and where they can help you. Be kind, be honest, and build the necessary rapport to make well developed products together.

Learning Activities

Practice:

- Connect with an instructional designer and learn about their day to day activities. Describe how they are similar or different from your own.

Reflection:

- Explain a typical day in your work. How do they translate into the day of an instructional designer?

Chapter 16

WHAT'S THE FUTURE OF INSTRUCTIONAL DESIGN?

The future of online course design is already here, but you just don't know it yet. We, as designers, are bombarded by new information daily and it's tough to decipher what is possible. I'm often asked in interviews to be a futurist and to predict what's the next big thing for instructional design. It's always funny when people mention radical ideas that they didn't think were possible, but I know that they do exist. For instance, I had a meeting with an educator the other day, and he mentioned trying to scale grading. There aren't enough instructors to do all of the grading, and he laughed saying "If only there was an algorithm where AI could accurately grade papers." I then told him that this product does exist and he could implement it into his courses right now. After looking at me like I had 3 heads, I explained about how I tested out a product years ago where the AI could be fed a substantial amount of papers, typical feedback, normal suggestions, and a rubric, and sure enough, the AI graded the papers pretty darn close compared to what the instructor would've done. This is the thing folks, these ideas exist, but it takes some time to find them, to vet them, and then of course, to properly implement them.

Trying to change how we have done something for years, such as designing courses, takes a slow and steady pace and the results may never come. This has led to some standards of course design that have become outdated, in my opinion. If you are an instructional designer or have taught online courses before, you've experienced this. We have all reviewed, or taught a course, or taken a course before where you are left with the thoughts of:

- Why are there so many discussion boards?
- Why are there 10 learning outcomes and they don't make sense?
- Why do the graphics of this video look straight out of 1997?
- Why does this ebook frame the information this way?

The thing is that we don't have to settle as designers. There are possibilities out there right now on how to make the course feel more human like and to focus our attention on our students.

As someone who is deeply invested into the instructional design community and have taught online for years, I've seen a few new ideas that have worked. I also am currently working on some of these ideas right now, and while I don't have the data for all of them to support my claims, I'm confident these ideas will become the new norm at some point in time. This is why I want to tell you about them now to help prepare you for the future. It's also entirely possible for an interviewer to ask you about your thoughts on the future of designing courses.

Get ready for the future because this is what I'm predicting will happen with future online courses:

Designated Learner Check-Ins

My big lesson from 2020 is that it's okay to not be okay. I taught online graduate courses all throughout 2020 and witnessed the impact the state of the world had on my students. They wrote about heartache and troubles in the discussion board and would reach out to me via email about their situations. Like clockwork, the email would always start off with an apology. "I'm sorry Dr. Hobson, but I won't be able to submit my assignment because my mother is in the hospital" or "I was just let go by my employer." Whatever the case was, there was never a need for an apology due to a life altering event. While I posted in my announcements and sent emails telling students to please never fret about these issues, they always worried. It wasn't until "check-ins" were designed into my courses that I started to notice a difference.

These check-in sessions were either video recordings or written submissions where the students could explain about what they went through for the week and if they had any questions on the course content. While many of my students sent check-ins saying everything was fine and that they had no questions, I did start to notice a trend. Students were opening up more. They celebrated their wins like how one student told me she accepted a job offer because of the knowledge she gained from the MBA program. They also talked about their struggles. Sometimes, it was around the course content, but most times, it was around time management, stress, or the unknown. The check-ins created a new private communication channel directly to me and these check-ins even informed me with how their performance was going to be for the next few weeks. As an instructor, it let me know each of these students and to provide the best way to support their individual needs.

The only caveat to this idea is that it took a substantial amount of time each week to go through each video and written submission. If your plan is to incorporate these check-ins into your courses, make sure to provide a buffer for the instructor with their time commitments. Something has to come off their plates if you are going to be making this a standard.

Peer-Reviewed Assignments

Students care what their instructors think. That's one of the main drivers for course sales is to learn from the best. What about to learn from each other though? For a living, I design online courses for adult students and the more I research their wants/needs, the more I hear about their desire to learn from one another. They hold their professors in a high regard, but they want to hear from people on their level and to see what they are doing. They don't necessarily want to work together in a group, but they want a way to share ideas and feedback. Enter in peer-graded assignments.

The concept of peer-reviewed assignments is relatively simple: let your peers review your work and give you a score. I've used these in my own courses, and students always find this idea to be mind-blowing. What I see happen every time I use this is that students need to use their critical thinking skills with grading an assignment using a rubric. They are now the ones in the driver seat as help their peers. The best part of all is how receptive they are to one another's feedback. It's one thing to have constant comments come from an instructor. It's another thing to have their peers, who are going through the same experience with them, provide feedback.

Something that was incredible to witness was when two students from the same organization, working at different locations, were in the same class together. This was a course based around manufacturing and they happened to submit their assignments on a problem they were dealing with at each of their locations. Upon reading each other's assignments, it sparked an idea that led to a new protocol for the entire organization. They began to brainstorm in the discussion board and other students from similar companies described how they approached comparable issues. If it wasn't for this peer-reviewed assignment, this collaboration would've never happened. Unfortunately, as more organizations grow, it means that there are more isolated incidents with employees at different locations not knowing what others are going through. The platform gave them the opportunity to connect and they used it to the best of their capabilities.

XR/VR Representation

There is a delicate balance between wanting students to have their cameras turned on during courses and also understanding how annoying it is to be on camera for so many hours a day. With my life being Zoom for the last year, if there is an opportunity to not have my camera turned on, I'm taking it. I've been telling my students to do what they are comfortable with, but what if there was a happy medium? I think there is and it's XR.

XR is short for extended reality and this is the umbrella term for referring to real-and-virtual combined environments. I've been working on a new XR course lately for MIT and the professor mentioned "V Tubers." I sat there completely puzzled wondering "What is a V Tuber?" I'll assume you have never heard of this either so allow me to explain. V Tubers are virtual YouTubers who use XR to portray an animated character to be on camera instead of their actual faces. There are several variations of this with V Tubers using anime characters, animals, or a life-like virtual appearance of themselves. I tried this and created a 3D version of myself that captured my every motions and mannerisms to make it feel like I was genuinely speaking on camera. The only difference was that it made me, as the user, feel more comfortable with being on camera and I could relax a bit. This is what I'm thinking that students need. It's a way to participate on their own terms, without feeling like they're forced to watch their every movement on camera.

There are actually a number of ways to do this and a quick Google search will show you different options like Steam, Ready Player Me, FaceRig, VRoid Studio, and more. They all have their own pros and cons, operating system preferences, and different costs, but you can figure out the best options for you and your students. I could honestly see a day where an instructor is hosting a student webinar and the audience view would be a mix of virtual characters and people in real time.

Another fantastic resource that falls into this world is GatherTown. I was first introduced to GatherTown when I went to a virtual conference. To start, I had to make an avatar, and then I moved around a virtual world to find the room with the keynote speaker. After searching a bit, I found where he was sat and then sat down in a chair to have a link be sent with the video call. After the speech was over, I was able to explore around other areas of the conference and it felt so real. The closer I moved towards other people, the louder the conversation became. When I was close enough to others to fully hear them, a video panel appeared. Think of Zoom embedded into Super Mario. This dialogue option was proximity based so if I wanted to back out of the conversation, I could move my character away. This also allowed for private conversations to happen with similar ideas to breakout rooms. GatherTown provided a fun learning experience in an age where we are all tired of non-stop Zoom calls.

A Standard for Additional Resources

Our new normal is evolving and students are going to expect us to pull out all the stops. What I'm predicting is that the "additional resources" section in courses is going to expand to uncharted waters. This hunch comes from my own courses where incorporating podcasts has become a standard. In the courses I designed, I've made podcasts to follow along with the content. In the courses I've taught, I've found podcasts that align to each week. For instance, when I teach my marketing course and we cover the week on SEO, I'll find a podcast that interviews an expert on SEO. I've been able to do this with every subject in marketing and other areas as well.

Now is the time to listen to what our students are expecting from our designs. Think about every obstacle universities experienced with remote learning. What these instructors, administrators, and students went through isn't wasted effort. It was a learning process. We can take away those lessons and apply them towards a new future. Let's use an example with recorded lecture material. While the recorded sessions may or may not be of the best quality, it's what we can do with these to transform them to a better resource. Imagine taking the transcript from a recorded lecture from a course and turning this into a well-designed handout for students to download. What if multiple recorded lecturers could become a series of blog posts or an ebook? What's to stop us from stripping the audio and editing them with video animations to make them become enjoyable shorts on YouTube? Students can have access to any of these pieces of content ahead of time to come more prepared to class or view them once class is over to help reinforce the content. This isn't a battle of in-person vs online, but rather we have an opportunity to enhance both.

There are so many possibilities of what you can do with existing material to transform them in a way that future students can enjoy. The key is to not just repurpose this material into a different format, but to go the extra mile to make the content enjoyable and deeper the learning experience. So, what will the additional resources section look like? Blogs, podcasts, YouTube videos, games, are a few educated guesses. Another significant additional resource could be combining industry standard certificates into the classroom. If I was making a course right now in the IT field, I would research any way to have the material align with Google Certificates. The same thing could be said with a project management course and PMP certification or a cybersecurity program and Certified Information Systems Security Professional (CISSP) certification. The combination of industry experience and education will lead to many more opportunities for students.

Flexibility to Complete Coursework

This topic is quite a complicated one to do, but it can be done. For many instructional designers and educators, the goal is to be able to let students choose their own learning path. How do you want your students to show what they've learned? Perhaps an essay, a slide deck, a video, or a written proposal? How about we let them decide. This is taking Universal Design for Learning (UDL) and Competency-Based Education (CBE) and mashing them together. As an instructor, I like to prepare my students for what they are going to experience in the workplace. Most of my courses revolve around leadership, which means that there is a time and place for demonstrating different skills. To give you an example, imagine being the director of social media team. Under your watch, an intern mistakenly sent out a test email to all of the paying customers for your product. How do you handle the situation? There are a few stakeholders you need to address to resolve the problem. The first is obviously the paying customers who received the confusing test email. The second is your internal team and supervisor. To the customers, it makes sense to submit another email to diffuse the situation so writing skills would obviously be necessary here. At the same time, you are going to have to explain your next steps in a meeting to the internal team about what happened and what you propose moving forwards, meaning that your public speaking skills will be tested.

I would rather let my students pick and choose how they would handle this situation and then to work with others to see what they would do and to have a better understanding of all perspectives. This scenario actually happened within HBO. An intern accidentally submitted an email called, 'Integration Test Email #1" to most of their paying customers and HBO started to immediately trend on twitter. Their team responded in an amazing fashion saying, "We mistakenly sent out an empty test email to a portion of our HBO Max mailing list this evening. We apologize for the inconvenience, and as the jokes pile in, yes, it was the intern. No, really. And we're helping them through it." It received 162K likes and was shared for their humility and humor with how they addressed the issue.

For most situations, there are usually different options on how to solve the problem, and I would rather let my students decide which method they would choose and then tell me the reasoning behind it. I understand this isn't always true with every subject, but the idea of letting an adult make their decision and justify their actions is a learning experience. I wish there was an easy way for me to describe to you on how to do this within your organization and with your platform. Some can already do this, for others, it's complicated or entirely not possible. I've seen it work, and I know it can be done. Do your research on this one because it's a doozy, but it's worth it.

Once again, these are all ideas that can be done today, but more research is needed on how to make them as efficient as possible. All of this shows though that the industry is breaking new ground and it's such an exciting time to be an instructional designer.

▓ Learning Activities

Practice:

- Conduct your own research on where instructional design is heading. Find one topic that you are passionate about and describe how it could impact your design process.

Reflection:

- If you had to envision online learning 10 years from now, what does it look like?

Chapter 17

WHAT'S YOUR RECOMMENDATION ON...?

This chapter is a little bit different from all of the rest, but I knew when writing this book that it had to be in here somewhere. When it comes to online learning or any passion project for that matter, people want the insider secrets. They want to know about the benefits of products and services that can help them and solve their problems. While being an instructional designer, I've had to provide my own recommendations on several different topics, and that's what this chapter is all about. Whether you are looking for your next learning platform or what university's program to attend, I've listed all of my recommendations like a catalog in this chapter. To be transparent, many of the links below are a part of affiliate programs and your purchases help support my efforts. So, a big thank you if you purchase through my links.

In no particular order here are my recommendations:

Instructional Design Degree

An instructional design degree isn't necessary in our field, but chances are that having one will help you. If you wish to go back to school, I would recommend Bloomsburg University. Bloomsburg offers an MS in Instructional Design and Technology as well as ID certificates. To hear more about their benefits and the benefits of an instructional design degree in general, listen to my episode with Dr. Karl Kapp from Bloomsburg University.

Corporate Training

For corporate training and professional development, I recommend IDOL Courses Academy. Dr. Robin Sargent has built an incredible training program that has helped instructional designers land jobs at organizations like Google, General Motors, and Amazon. She's become a great friend of mine over the years and I know her trainings can accelerate your career in corporate instructional design. Listen to her podcast episode about the benefits of IDOL.

Freelance Training

For many people, the notion of being your own boss is the dream. It's a worthwhile dream, but it sure is challenging to do! You need the right guidance in place to start your business and to help with your development. For freelance trainings, I turn to Dr. Nicole Papiannou Lugara's Your Instructional Designer. Dr. Papaioannou Lugara also came on the podcast to talk about her lessons for new instructional designers on what to say to hiring managers.

Higher Education Training

For professional development in higher education, I'd recommend my product called Instructional Design Institute. I created the institute for new and entry level instructional designers in higher education. Within the institute are courses, webinars, and a community to support your needs.

Podcast Equipment/Software

Thinking about starting your own podcast? You are going to need the right equipment and software to get the job done. For a microphone, I'd recommend the ATR-2100. It plugs directly into your USB port and sounds great without any effects. To record my podcasts, I use Squadcast. You will also want an RSS feed to connect your podcast to Apple, Spotify, and other platforms. For this, I'd recommend to use

Libsyn. To edit your podcasts, you can use Garageband or Audacity.

Graphic Design Software

While instructional designers aren't graphic designers, we can be asked to help in this area. Depending upon your skill level, I have two different recommendations. If you are new to graphic design or need a project done quickly, I'd recommend Canva. If you would like to use a more sophisticated tool or have an extensive project, I'd recommend Adobe Photoshop.

Video Editing Software

Depending upon the size and scope of the project changes my recommendation for which tool to use when it comes to video editing. Many instructional designers swear by Camtasia for its simplicity and elegance. For more complicated projects, you might want to look at Adobe Premiere and Adobe After Effects. If you have watched my YouTube videos, these are the tools I use to edit my videos.

Learning Platform

Whether you are working in corporate or higher education, I would recommend Eduflow as your learning platform. I have used just about every LMS you can think of and Eduflow is the best in my opinion. Their platform is easy to build on and looks amazing. They also have assessments and tools to create a unique learning experience for your students. When you sign up with Eduflow, be sure to use my discount code (DRLUKEHOBSON) to save you 10% off of your subscription.

Instructional Design Books

Even though you are reading an instructional design book, I certainly have more recommendations! *Design for How People Learn* by Julie Dirksen is basically the Bible of instructional designers. Right behind this book though is Tim Slade's *the Elearning Designer's Handbook*. Either option will certainly help!

Books on Learning

I have so many recommendations for books on specifically learning so it was hard not to recommend all of them. If I had to pick my top three though, they would be *How Learning Works* by Ambrose et al., *Make it Stick* by Brown et al., and *UDL & Blended Learning* by Dr. Katie Novak and Dr. Caitlin Tucker. Any of these will help take your knowledge on learning to the next level.

Website Builder

If you are looking to build your own brand or create a website for your portfolio, I'd recommend <u>Squarespace</u>. What I love about Squarespace is that you can find a template for just about anything and make it your own.

Business / Entrepreneurship

There are endless possibilities out there for entrepreneurs in education. The problem is that it's a humungous headache trying to organize everything under one roof. I've found <u>Kajabi</u> to be a lifesaver when it comes to condensing everything into one platform. Kajabi can help with products, websites, landing pages, payments, analytics, marketing automations, email, communities, and more.

Simulations

In my courses, I love to use simulations. The key to using simulations though is that they have to be outstanding or else students won't use them. For my courses, I use the simulations by <u>Harvard Business Publishing Education</u>. They have a simulation for just about any subject you could need.

Free Education

Let's say you want to learn about a subject from one of the top institutions in the world for free. How would you go about doing this? The answer is <u>MIT's OCW</u>. You can find course materials, lectures, and notes on any nerdy subject and best of all, it's free.

YouTube Channels

YouTube has become one of the trusted platforms to learn more about instructional design. The channels I recommend to check out our <u>Devlin Peck</u>, <u>Tim Slade</u>, <u>Vanessa Anchored</u>, <u>Alex Mitts</u>, <u>Cara North</u>, and <u>Anna Sabramowicz</u>. Of course, if you haven't already, <u>be sure to check out mine too</u>.

ELearning Blogs

If you are like me, you first learned about instructional design from blogs. It was actually the inspiration behind <u>starting my own</u>. When I think of instructional design blogs, three bloggers to mind: <u>Devlin Peck</u>, <u>Connie Malamed</u>, and <u>Christy Tucker</u>. All of these websites are packed with fantastic instructional design goodness that will keep you engaged for days!

Podcasts

It's no secret that I'm obsessed with podcasts so I had to mention a few in here! <u>Dear Instructional Designer</u> by Kristen Anthony stopped making episodes years ago, but this to me is the original ID podcast. <u>I'm New Here</u> by Nyla Spooner is a fantastic introduction podcast for those new to the field. <u>The eLearning Coach</u> by Connie Malamed has been around since 2013 and covers just about any topic in ID that you can think of. To learn more from an instructor perspective, I'd highly recommend <u>Lecture Breakers</u> by Dr. Barbi Honeycutt. There are many more you can find by searching "Instructional Design Podcasts" on Google or Apple Podcasts.

Chapter 18

CONCLUSION

When I started to write this book, I kept on thinking about what I wish I knew before becoming an instructional designer. Every experience and life lesson became another chapter. I started to become obsessed with sharing as much as I could with you and it's been difficult to say when this book should end. I feel like I could write a never-ending story to help you along this learning journey, but practically speaking, there has to be a close.

As I started to outline the conclusion, I pondered about why I wanted to be an instructional designer in the first place. What was it that made me not give up trying to become an instructional designer when I was told repeatedly that it wasn't the right fit for me? It simply might've been those rejections because when someone tells me that I can't do something, a burning desire fills me wanting to prove the doubters wrong. That's not my purpose though.

At the beginning of every podcast episode and YouTube video, I say that my purpose is to help you make online learning experience meaningful for you and for your students. That's why I wanted to become an instructional designer so badly. I didn't want other students out there to go through a miserable learning experience. I want the next generation to be introduced to a whole new kind of thinking when it comes to education. Instead of kids saying that school is boring, I envision a world where they want to better themselves through knowledge. Instead of adults dreading having to do mandatory trainings, I want them to experience an online course so incredible that they share it on social media. Instead of college students thinking that face-to-face learning is the only way to learn, I want them to make online learning their preferred option. I just want to make this world a better place through education.

My way of doing this was through this book. It was to give you a fighting chance of making it in this field and being able to pass it along to the next up and coming instructional designers. It was Mother Theresa who said, "I alone cannot change the world, but I can cast a stone across the waters to create many ripples." I care about impacting your career and the careers of the next wave of instructional designers. The trajectory of our field is unlike anything I've seen before and in a few years from now, it's entirely possible for kids to say when they grow up, they want to be an instructional designer. This might be wishful thinking, but I'll choose this optimistic point of view.

For my final thoughts, as you grow in your career, take this journey one step at a time. You're going to make mistakes and that's okay. That's how you learn. Every experience is a small piece to the puzzle we call life. I've certainly made plenty of mistakes in my career, but I didn't dwell on them. I chose to view them as an opportunity to get better each time. I still have this mindset and always will. You'll never stop learning as long as you live and as long as you are willing to listen. Carry this growth mindset with you as you explore each opportunity and your online learning experiences for your students will be unbelievable.

And that folks is everything I wish I knew before becoming an instructional designer.

Made in the USA
Monee, IL
07 September 2023

42357603R00122